CORNELL STUDIES IN PHILOSOPHY

No. 3

D0808694

THE PHILOSOPHY

OF

FRIEDRICH NIETZSCHE

BY

GRACE NEAL DOLSON, A.B., Ph.D.

Professor of Philosophy in Wells College

New York
THE MACMILLAN COMPANY
1901

PREFACE.

The aim of this monograph is to give a critical exposition of Nietzsche's writings, in so far as they are concerned with philosophy, and at the same time to point out their historical position. According to Riehl,[1] no modern German writer of the more earnest class is so widely read as Nietzsche. There has been, and still is in many quarters, a tendency to make light of his writings, and to regard him as a philosophical charlatan who had come to take himself seriously; but his influence is too great to make such an easy explanation allowable. One may hesitate to ratify the claims made by his disciples on his behalf, and so place him among the foremost thinkers of all time; but he is, and will probably remain a significant figure among the philosophers of the last quarter of the nineteenth century. At present he is much in vogue in Germany and France, especially with readers who have not had philosophical training, and the fashion is spreading to England and America. Criticisms, reviews, and 'appreciations' follow one another in rapid succession, and there must be a reason for their number. In some way Nietzsche appeals to the thought of the time, and so great a success can hardly be due to pretence.

Doubtless a portion of the attention accorded to his writings has been given to them from anything but friendly motives. The theologians have felt called upon to refute his arguments against religion in general, and to show the lack of historical proof for his account of the origin of Christianity. They have answered his scorn, which naturally provoked them more than his objections, by applying to him all manner of opprobrious epithets. He has figured as Antichrist and as the devil's prophet, not to mention other interesting but less important personages. Such vigorous opposition has, of course, had its share in making Nietzsche well known; and when it is joined to the

[1] *Friedrich Nietzsche. Der Künstler und der Denker*, p. 14.

more temperate criticisms provoked by his theories concerning morality, the combined effect of the two has been no small matter. It is impossible to ignore a man who laughs at all that many people deem holy.

The attention accorded to Nietzsche, however, is too widespread to be altogether accounted for by the opposition that he has awakened. Besides, much of it is favorable to his doctrines. He has had imitators and admirers in abundance. Novels have been written setting forth his theories, *e. g.*, *Seine Gottheit*, by Emil Marriot, and *Also sprach Zarathustra's Sohn*, by Otto v. Leixner. Richard Strauss has composed some program music, entitled, *Also sprach Zarasthustra*. The entire literary movement known as Young Germany acknowledges his leadership; and his influence is apparent in many recently published books treating of the social problem. *Also sprach Zarathustra* has already reached its twelfth edition. The Macmillans have in preparation an English translation of his collected works, of which three volumes have already been published; and if the signs of the times may be trusted, America, at least, and probably England, too, will soon join the ranks of the countries where Nietzsche is widely read.

All this, however, would hardly entitle Nietzsche to a place in the history of philosophic thought. To justify his claims there, more than opposition or popularity is necessary; and such careful studies as those of Alois Riehl and Henri Lichtenberger show that he has met with attention also from men well fitted to judge the philosophical value of his work. These two, as well as other men of the profession, regard Nietzsche as worthy of serious consideration; and whether they have agreed with him or not, they have admitted his claim to serious discussion and criticism.

In fact, Nietzsche is no isolated phenomenon. In the last chapter of this study an attempt has been made to show that his system is a part of the general intellectual movement of the past decades, and the attention which his views have received seem to confirm that view. In one sense, he was inevitable. He expresses clearly and forcibly what many people have thought; and the fact that he is more radical than most of them only adds to his charm. The man who is on the same road, but goes a

step further than one has dared to go oneself, exercises an irre-
sistible fascination.   Add to this the magic of Nietzsche's style,
and there is reason enough for his increasing popularity.

G. N. D.

WELLS COLLEGE, AURORA,
December 22, 1900.

TABLE OF CONTENTS.

PAGE.

Chapter I. INTRODUCTION 1–18

Section 1. Biography... 1
" 2. General Nature of the System......................... 12

Chapter II. THE ÆSTHETIC PERIOD...................................19–33

Section 1. General Characteristics 19
" 2. Theories of Art and Culture......................... 23

Chapter III. THE INTELLECTUAL PERIOD........................... 34–62

Section 1. Truth... 35
" 2. Culture 47
" 3. Æsthetics.. 50
" 4. Religion 51
" 5. Ethics 56

Chapter IV. THE ETHICAL PERIOD 63–84

Section 1. Truth.. 63
" 2. Religion, especially Christianity....................... 66
" 3. The Derivation of Morality .....,................... 68
" 4. Responsibility and Punishment....................... 75
" 5. The Moral Ideal—Fulness of Life *versus* Degeneration... 77
" 6. The Over-man and the Eternal Recurrence......... 80

CHAPTER V. NIETZSCHE'S RELATION TO OTHER WRITERS AND HIS SIGNIFICANCE....................................85–103

Section 1. Schopenhauer 85
" 2. Hegel and the Hegelians....................... 92
" 3. The Materialistic and the Neo-Kantian Movements 93
" 4. Literary Affinities 95
" 5. Nietzsche's Significance................................. 97

BIBLIOGRAPHY.......................... 104

CHAPTER I.

INTRODUCTION.

Sec. 1. Biography.

IT is a misfortune for the writer of a sketch, however brief, of the life of Friedrich Nietzsche, that the biography by his sister is not yet completed. Two volumes have already been published, which bring the hero down to the year 1880, shortly after he resigned his professorship at Bâle. Although sometimes wearisome in its minuteness, this account of Nietzsche by the person who knew him best, brings its own justification with it. His sister revered him as a genius whose lightest word was worthy of preservation, as a being so exalted that no falsification could place him higher, to whom truth and truth alone was due. Even as a child, she collected his chance writings, and rescued many interesting bits from the waste-paper basket. Her biography is full of these and of household anecdotes, which show us the personality of Nietzsche as nothing else could. We may regret that so many immature attempts at philosophy and æsthetics have been given to the public; it is an injustice to Nietzsche himself. But Frau Förster-Nietzsche expressly states[1] that the book is intended for those who love and reverence her brother, who share in the feelings with which she has written. Those who do not come under this category, may satisfy themselves with the brief accounts now to be found in such abundance.

Friedrich Wilhelm Nietzsche[2] was born at Röcken near Lützen, on the 15th of October, 1844. His father was a country pastor, and according to both Nietzsche and his sister, was a model of the Christian virtues. He was much beloved by his parishioners, a favorite in all social gatherings, and was especially gifted[3] in music. Although he died in 1849, as the result of a fall, his memory seems to have exercised great influence upon his

[1] *Das Leben Friedrich Nietzsche's*, Vol. I, *Vorrede*, p. viii.
[2] *Ibid.*, p. 5.
[3] *Ibid.*, p. 6.

children.   According to family tradition,[1] he was the descendant
of Polish nobles, who had been obliged by religious persecution
to flee from their own country.   The original form of the name
was Niëtzky.   The son Friedrich was always proud of his Polish
blood, and was often supposed by strangers to be a Pole.   There
were two other children, one of whom, also a boy, died while
still almost a baby.   The other was Elizabeth, the author of the
biography.   Both she and Friedrich seem to have inherited good
constitutions; in fact, the members of the family on both sides
were unusually long-lived.

In 1850, shortly after the death of the father, the family removed to Naumburg on the Saale.   The household was composed of mother, grandmother, two maiden aunts, and the two
children.   In this superabundance of feminine influence during
his early years, Ola Hannson [2] finds the cause of the low valuation that Nietzsche later placed upon women.   Be that as it may,
the combination of home surroundings and the conservative atmosphere at Naumburg, which at that time [3] was a stronghold
of church and state, probably had much to do with making
Nietzsche the queer old-fashioned child he was.   The other boys
at the common school teased him on account of his seriousness,
and called him the "little pastor."   Wonderful stories were told
of the moving way in which he could recite hymns and texts
from the Bible.

After a year at the common school, he was sent to a private
school until 1854, when he entered the Gymnasium.   Here he
displayed great love for solitude,[4] and his intercourse with the
other boys was limited almost entirely to two friends, who played
a large part in his early life.   In his school work he showed so
much talent, that he was given a free scholarship at Pforta,[5] a

[1] *Op. cit.*, p. 10.   Achelis in *Friedrich Nietzsche*, pp. 9 and 10, regards the
latter's Slavish descent as of great influence upon his character.   For instance, to that
is due his dreamy melancholy mixed with the bitterest hate, his scorn of the masses,
and his admiration for brute force, together with his tendency to belittle every rule of
life based upon reason.

[2] *Friedrich Nietzsche, seine Persönlichkeit und sein System*, pp. 6, 7.

[3] *Das Leben Friedrich Nietsche's*, I, p. 24.

[4] *Ibid.*, p. 32.

[5] *Ibid.*, p. 90.

famous boarding-school in the neighborhood. There he was a
model pupil[1] until he reached the *Obersecunda*, when he became
careless and thought of devoting himself entirely to music.
The school wearied him. Later, as the time for his final exam-
inations approached, he went to work again, but could not altogether make up for the time he had lost. He would have failed,
if his work in Latin and German had not been so good that it
was allowed to counterbalance his deficiencies in mathematics.
About four years before this,[2] he and his two friends formed
themselves into a little society for mutual culture. They held
regular meetings, to which each was supposed to contribute some
original work, which the others criticised. For the first year
and a half, they occupied themselves chiefly with poetry and
musical composition. Later, they decided to broaden their activities, lest they should become one-sided. In addition to this society, of which he was the most enthusiastic member, Nietzsche
devoted much of his leisure to reading and to the study of music.

In October, 1864, he entered the University of Bonn,[3] as a
student of philology and theology, the latter of which he dis-
continued at the end of the semester. During this first winter
of freedom, he spent more money than his allowance, chiefly for
music, the theatre, and little pleasure excursions. He joined one
of the student societies, but soon decided that he wanted none
of their "beer sociability." Possibly his disgust was partly
caused by the fact that he tried to improve their mode of life, and
failed. He said later[4] that people who had to drink beer and
smoke every night, were absolutely incapable of understanding
him. As a result of the year spent at Bonn, he attained greater
freedom and independence,[5] and was still further confirmed in his
decision to study philology. It seemed to him to offer a counter-
weight to his restless desire for all kinds of culture, and to promise
results without making too great demands upon his emotional
nature.

The removal of Ritschl, the philologian, from Bonn to Leipsic,

[1] *Op. cit.*, p. 165.
[2] *Ibid.*, pp. 132, 133.
[3] *Ibid.*, p. 199.
[4] *Ibid.*, p. 224.
[5] *Ibid.*, p. 210.

caused Nietzsche to change universities also, and he remained in Leipsic from October, 1865 until August, 1867.[1] He then began his term of military service, as a member of the mounted artillery in Naumburg. A few months later, he fell from his horse, injuring his breast bone so severely as to cause an illness of several months' duration, and to incapacitate him for further service. During his enforced leisure, he busied himself with philosophical studies[2] and with an index[3] to the twenty-four volumes of the *Rheinisches Museum*, which, on Ritschl's recommendation, had been entrusted to him. In the autumn of 1868, he returned to Leipsic to continue his studies, without, however, becoming a member of the University. His philological work had already taken on a philosophical tone. In fact, during the whole of his student life, the chief factors in his thinking were his interest in philology and his devotion to Schopenhauer. He had found by chance one day, in an antiquarian shop, *Die Welt als Wille und Vorstellung,* and, contrary to his habit, had carried it home with him.[4] This was the beginning of his Schopenhauer worship. He succeeded in inspiring his friends with the same feeling, and they formed a little coterie of devotees, reading Schopenhauer by day and dreaming of him by night. If one was in trouble, the others suggested appropriate passages. Nietzsche himself regarded his idol as a friend rather than as a book. If Schopenhauer had not been dead, he would certainly have attempted to come into some personal relationship with him. As it was, he had to content himself with endowing Schopenhauer with all the virtues of the ideal philosopher, probably with more satisfactory results than would have attended an acquaintance in the flesh.

In 1869, upon Ritschl's recommendation, Nietzsche was appointed to the professorship of classical philology at Bâle, although he was not yet twenty-five years of age, and had no degree.[5] The University of Leipsic promptly made him a doctor of philosophy without a thesis or examination,[6] and 'in May[7] of

[1] *Op. cit.*, p. 225.
[2] *Ibid.*, p. 269.
[3] *Ibid.*, p. 274.
[4] *Ibid.*, p. 231.
[5] *Ibid.*, p. 296.
[6] *Ibid.*, p. 301.
[7] *Ibid.*, II, p. 5.

the same year, he delivered his introductory address at Bâle. The young professor was most kindly received, but the appointment was in one way injurious to him. It necessitated an enormous amount of work, often far beyond his strength ; and without doubt much of his later ill health was caused by the over exertion of this period. Scarcely a year later he was made professor *ordinarius*.[1]

In 1870, Nietzsche went with the Prussian army as a volunteer nurse, since the declared neutrality of Switzerland made it impossible for him to serve as a soldier.[2] He soon became ill and had to return home, but not until the war had made a profound impression upon his sensitive mind. Before his health was fully restored, he went back to his work. During the following winter, he was obliged to take a vacation, which he spent in Italy. Later in the same year, he published *Die Geburt der Tragödie*, the first of his writings to be later included in his collected works. What he had done previously had been of a strictly philological nature, and had never extended beyond the limits of a magazine article. The *Geburt*[3] was much praised by his friends, but was viewed with suspicion by the philologians, and entirely ignored by the reviewers. He was too proud to defend his position, although he felt the hostile attitude keenly. Students at other universities were advised not to go to Bâle, and during the winter semester of '72–73, there were no philologians there at all. The pupils whom he did have, both then and later, seem to have held him in great honor. In 1873,[4] he published the first of the *Unzeitgemässe Betrachtungen*, namely, that directed against Strauss. The original plan included twenty-four such *Betrachtungen*,[5] only four of which were ever finished. The other three appeared shortly after the first. About this time he began to have that exaggerated opinion of his own intellect

---

[1] *Op. cit.*, II, p. 29.
[2] *Ibid.*, p. 33.
[3] *Ibid.*, p. 68.
[4] *Ibid.*, p. 127.
[5] *Ibid.*, p. 138. See also *Werke*, X, pp. 253–425, which contain the original sketches. All references to Nietzsche's works are to the standard edition published by Naumann.

which later became so painfully marked ; or, according to his sister, he first began to realize what a great man he was.[1] He thought several times [2] of giving up his professorship, in order to devote himself entirely to writing, but was persuaded not to do so by his friends in Bâle. In the winter of '77–'78 [3] he published the first volume of *Menschliches allzu Menschliches*, and a year later [4] *Vermischte Meinungen und Sprüche*. These books expressed a radical change of standpoint, and were received coldly even by Nietzsche's friends.

It was during this period that Nietzsche's friendship with Wagner was formed. Nietzsche had long been an admirer of Wagner's music, and once, during his residence in Leipsic, had met Wagner personally. After he went to Bâle, the acquaintance was renewed, and became the warmest of friendships. At that time, Wagner was living at Tribschen near Lucerne, and Nietzsche made him frequent visits there. After the first of these visits Nietzsche described Wagner in a letter to a friend as the image of Schopenhauer's genius. " No one knows him and can judge him," he goes on to say, " because all the world stands upon a different basis, and is not at home in his atmosphere. In him such an unconditioned ideality rules, such a deep and touching humanity, that I feel in his neighborhood as if I were near the divine." [5] " All the best and most beautiful for me," he writes elsewhere, " is bound together with the names of Schopenhauer

---

[1] *Das Leben Friedrich Nietzsche's*, II, p. 134. Expressions of this feeling are especially common in the later works, *e. g.*, *Der Fall Wagner*, *Werke*, VIII, p. 44. " I have given the Germans the deepest books that they possess;" and *Götzendämmerung*, *Werke*, VIII, p. 165. " I have given mankind the deepest book that it possesses, my *Zarathustra*. I shall give it shortly the most independent." Rudolf Steiner maintains (*Friedrich Nietzsche*. *Ein Kämpfer gegen seine Zeit*) that Nietzsche means no more than that he has dared to write a book whose contents were fetched deeper from the nature of a personality than is the case in similar books; and that by independence, he understands only independence of foreign judgment. This, according to Steiner. is modesty, inasmuch as it shows that Nietzsche regards his opinions as an expression of his own personality, and not as objective truth.

[2] *Das Leben Friedrich Nietzsche's*, II, p. 171.

[3] *Ibid.*, p. 289.

[4] *Ibid.*, p. 320.

[5] *Ibid.*, II, p. 13.

and Wagner." [1]   He regarded Wagner as the "master," and his music as the beginning of a new art.   He longed to do something for the cause, and the present form of the *Geburt*,[2] in place of the much more comprehensive work he had at first planned, is the expression of this desire.   After the Wagners had moved to Bayreuth, and the Bayreuth plan was threatening to be a failure,[3] Nietzsche laid aside his work upon the *Philosophy of the Greeks in the Tragic Age*, and, finding the cause of the German hostility to Wagner to lie in the condition of German culture, he made an example of Strauss.   Soon after this, the relationship between the two men, although outwardly the same, began to be of a somewhat different nature.[4]   Nietzsche's writings ceased to please Wagner.   Each found that the other was not in complete agreement with him.   Wagner was not so lovable [5] "in the world," as he had been in retirement at Tribschen; and Nietzsche suspected that the "master" wished to deprive every one of intellectual freedom. [6]   The *Betrachtung, Richard Wagner in Bayreuth* was a farewell.[7]   Nietzsche felt that all was over between him and Wagner, and was extremely unhappy over the breach between them.   Wagner [8] had almost taken the place of his dead father, and he regarded Wagner's wife as the foremost woman of the time.   The only differences between the two men seem to have been those of opinion.   Nietzsche had ceased to find in the Wagnerian music the hope of all future art; but for a time he believed it possible that Wagner might see his mistake, and the friendship might be preserved.   In 1876,[9] he went to Bayreuth for the rehearsals and the first opera season, but did not stay long.   Wagner treated him with special honor, but Nietzsche did not attempt to conceal his real feelings.   According to Frau Förster-Nietzsche,[10] the separation seemed sudden, only because Nietzsche had not seen Wagner for two years, and had not heard

---

[1] *Op. cit.*, p. 18.

[2] *Ibid.*, p. 46.   See also *Werke*, IX, pp. 25–182.

[3] *Ibid.*, p. 126.   See also *Werke*, X, pp. 1–157.

[4] *Ibid.*, p. 144.   [8] *Ibid.*, p. 206.

[5] *Ibid.*, p. 215.   [9] *Ibid.*, p. 243.

[6] *Ibid.*, p. 230.   [10] *Ibid.*, p. 260.

[7] *Ibid.*, p. 237.

his music given for four years. He had been quietly growing away from Wagner, and now saw how deceived he had been. He had read into Wagner his own ideas of the music of the future. In 1878, when the first volume of *Menschliches allzu Menschliches* was completed, he sent a copy to Wagner, who made no comment upon it.[1] At the same time Nietzsche received a copy of *Parsifal*, which he also passed over in silence.[2] After that there was no communication between them.

This friendship and its rupture was probably the most important event in Nietzsche's life. For a person whose mental experiences were so intense, perhaps no friendship was possible without intellectual agreement. Probably, too, the fact that Nietzsche took himself and his convictions so seriously made it necessary for him to give public expression to his changed attitude. Wagner seems to have been like him in this respect, and so perhaps their final separation was inevitable. One thing, however, no intensity of conviction can excuse, and that is the personal invective to which Nietzsche descends in *Der Fall Wagner* and *Nietzsche contra Wagner*. Here he shows himself in so unenviable a light, that it is difficult not to feel that, in the early quarrel, Wagner must have been the injured party.[3] The best and kindest course for the Nietzsche devotees is not to seek to excuse what is inexcusable, but, as nearly as may be, to pass the matter over in silence.

Of Nietzsche's other friendships the most important were those with Paul Rée, Georg Brandes, and Bernhard Cron, better known as Peter Gast. Rée spent the first winter in Italy with him,[4] and each seems to have found a keen intellectual stimulus in the other's society. The relation with Brandes was not so close, and found expression in correspondence rather than in personal intercourse. Peter Gast was more, or perhaps less than

---

[1] *Op. cit.*, p. 294.

[2] *Ibid.*, p. 297.

[3] According to Eugen Kretzer (*Friedrich Nietzsche. Nach persönlichen Erinnerungen und aus seinen Schriften*, pp. 17 and 18), a Wagnerian, Edward Kulke, in a book called *Richard Wagner und Friedrich Nietzsche*, says that Nietzsche left Wagner because the latter refused to produce an opera written by Nietzsche. This has been denied, says Kretzer, by people in a position to know.

[4] *Das Leben Friedrich Nietzsche's*, II, p. 276.

a friend ; he was a disciple,[1] and the only one Nietzsche thought
worthy of the name. No doubt the wandering life necessitated
by his illness hindered the formation of friendships after his removal from Bâle, but both then and earlier he was a most exact-
ing friend. So few people were capable of understanding him.
Any difference of opinion was interpreted as lack of appreciation,
and the subjects upon which he allowed slight deviations from
his own law and gospel were few. This may not have been altogether due to vanity or arrogance. Nietzsche believed and
doubted so devoutly that he made conviction or lack of it a
test of character. He could no more associate with a man who
held views opposed to his own, than four hundred years ago a
Catholic could make friends with a Protestant.

Perhaps because of this uncompromising tendency, Nietzsche
chose to spend much of his time in the society of women. [2] He
never married, but the tiny circle of Nietzsche-worshipers surrounding him numbered a succession of women, among them
some of the best known in Germany, for instance, Fräulein von
Meysenbug,[3] the author of *Memoiren einer Idealistin.* His sister
was the first and most ardent of these followers, and her influence
over him was undoubtedly great. Ola Hannson regards her
as an unusually gifted woman, with a mind bearing a decided
resemblance to that of her brother. Another of the devotees was
Frau Lou Andreas-Salomé, who since that time has written a
work of some two hundred fifty pages concerning Nietzsche's theories, personality, and intellectual development. Unfortunately
for the reliability of the book, Frau Förster-Nietzsche calls it a
falsification in all respects.[4] Her own account of the connection
between the two is as follows. Sometime during the '80's, it
was Nietzsche's wish to find a disciple who would preserve all
his philosophical remarks, even those uttered hastily. In the

[1] *Op. cit,* p. 239.

[2] Ola Hannson : *Friedrich Nietzsche, seine Persönlichkeit und sein System,* pp.
6, 7.

[3] *Das Leben Friedrich Nietzsche's,* II, pp. 274, 276.

[4] *Ibid., Vorrede,* pp. vii, viii. Frau Förster-Nietzsche's criticism of Frau Andreas-Salomé's book calls in question the interpretation of facts rather than the
facts themselves.

spring of 1882, Dr. Rée recommended Fräulein Lou Salomé, who possessed extraordinary gifts. Before long, however, Nietzsche came to the conclusion that the young woman understood nothing of him ; and after an acquaintance of five months, he broke off all intercourse with her.

In October, 1876, Nietzsche procured a year's leave of absence on account of ill health, and went to Italy.[1] The following winter he was again obliged to give up a portion of his work, and in the spring of 1879, shortly after publishing *Vermischte Meinungen und Sprüche*, he resigned his position altogether.[2] He had been professor at Bâle for ten years, and had not only done the work pertaining to his office, but had been unusually productive besides. During the latter part of this time, he had never been well for more than a few months, being troubled especially with pain in his head and eyes. He spent the following winter at Naumburg,[3] and after that went from one health resort to another, usually passing the winter at Geneva or Nice, the summers in the upper Engadine.[4] After 1882 his condition slightly improved, and he published book after book in rapid succession. In January, 1889, he became hopelessly insane and lived at his sister's home in Weimar most of the time until his death, which occurred on the twenty-fifth of August, 1900.[5]

There has been much difference of opinion as to the nature and extent of Nietzsche's illness. On the one hand, Max Nordau maintains, what is manifestly untrue, that all of Nietzsche's books were written between periods of residence in a mad-house.[6] More plausible, because not based upon evident misstatements, is the attempt by Hermann Türck to show that Nietzsche displayed unmistakeable signs of predisposition to insanity, and that his theories can be explained, only when they are regarded as the result of perverted instincts.[7] At the other extreme stands Frau

---

[1] *Op. cit.*, p. 274.
[2] *Ibid.*, p. 324.
[3] *Ibid.*, p. 335.
[4] Henri Lichtenberger : *La Philosophie de Nietzsche*, p. 80.
[5] *Ibid.*, p. 79 ff.
[6] *Degeneration*, English translation of the second German edition, pp. 452, 453.
[7] *Friedrich Nietzsche und seine philosophischen Irrwege, passim*, especially pp. 6–9.

Lou Andreas-Salomé, who, according to Nordau,[1] says that Nietzsche has gone into voluntary retirement from the world, because he could not endure to be so misunderstood. The truth seems to be that he showed no symptoms of insanity during the long period of his illness ;[2] and indeed, he speaks with astonishment of the entire lack of influence that his physical condition had upon his intellect. Of course, his own opinion upon the matter is not of as much value as that of an unprejudiced third person ; but in the absence of such unbiased testimony, it should not be disregarded. His sister says that he was in all respects the reverse of a nervous man.[3] Whatever one may think of Nietzsche's conclusions, his work certainly deserves careful consideration ; and any preconceived idea that it is the result of incipient madness, must necessarily vitiate such consideration. It is so easy to think that opinions differing radically from those commonly accepted bear the stamp of disease.

Another error that has been widely circulated,[4] makes Nietzsche's insanity the result of heredity, and finds traces of similar diseases on both sides of his family. On the contrary, as has already been stated, he seems to have come from remarkably good stock. The only circumstance that would at all seem to bear out the theory of heredity, is that his father died of concussion of the brain. This, however, was the direct consequence of a fall, and it is difficult to see how he could bequeath it to his children. Peter Gast,[5] who affirms that he is in a position to prove from family documents that Nietzsche had an excellent physical and mental inheritance, regards his insanity as due to protracted insomnia, and to the large amount of chloral prescribed by physicians to overcome it. Frau Förster-Nietzsche also says[6] that her brother undoubtedly injured his constitu-

---

[1] *Degeneration*, p. 456. No specific reference to the writings of Frau Lou Andreas-Salomé is given.

[2] Lichtenberger (*Friedrich Nietzsche, Aphorismes et Fragments Choisis*, Introduction, pp. iv, v) maintains that Nietzsche was in no respect abnormal, and that his writings do not display the anarchy of instincts characteristic of degeneration.

[3] *Das Leben Friedrich Nietzsche's*, II, p. 41.

[4] *Ola Hannson : Friedrich Nietzsche, seine Persönlichkeit und sein System*, p. 6.

[5] *Also sprach Zarathustra*, second edition, preface, footnote, pp. xxv–xxix.

[6] *Das Leben Friedrich Nietzsche's*, II, p. 46.

tion by frequent recourse to violent remedies. Lichtenberger,[1] on the other hand, while admitting the lack of evidence, says that the nature of Nietzsche's illness, so far as we know it, makes it difficult to discard entirely the hypothesis of hereditary influence. Nietzsche himself believed that he had received the germs of his disease from his father, and, at the time of his greatest suffering, in 1880, waited for the stroke that was to end everything for him. It never came, however—at least in the form in which he expected it. His own trouble was of an entirely different nature, one which, though not less fatal in its results, manifested itself more gradually.

Sec. 2. *General Nature of the System.*

It can hardly be said that Nietzsche has a philosophical system. With the exception of his earlier work, he has confined himself almost exclusively to the aphorism, which makes connected exposition impossible. Probably the choice of this form for the expression of his ideas was due to his shattered health, which forced him to do most of his work while walking in the open air ; but many stray comments upon La Rochefoucauld and other French writers show that he was not insensible to the advantages he had thereby gained. Although the aphorism is not adapted to systematic development of particular theories, and still less to the exposition of their mutual relationship, yet on the other hand, it lends itself better than any other style to the discussion of a wide range of topics. This quality of the aphorism Nietzsche made use of to the utmost. His philosophy included every subject that interested him. He found no difficulty in passing from a theory of the good to a description of secondary education. To some extent, in the catholicity of his interests he reminds one of the Greek philosophers. They, too, made of philosophy a sort of encyclopædia, not of facts, but of the views of the author. Like them, Nietzsche made use of all the phases of his experience. Whatever he met with, both in the physical and in the intellectual world, was given a place in his theory of life, and helped to give it its final form.

[1] *La Philosophie de Nietzsche*, p. 81.

The one unifying thought in all this mass of material gives a partial explanation of its very abundance. No matter how many different aspects Nietzsche's philosophy may present, however numerous the subjects it may embrace, it is always and everywhere a philosophy of culture.[1] Naturally, then, no questions of human life are foreign to it. The point of view of culture, though sometimes excluding other standpoints, looks with interest upon all possible objects. It is not entirely intellectual, nor æsthetic, nor moral. It does not even feel itself above the petty little details of manners, current events, and the like. A philosophy founded upon it loses in systematic form and in accuracy, but gains in breadth. Almost inevitably, too, such a philosophy ceases to become an abstraction, and becomes an expression of the personality of its author. Perhaps no opinion can be entirely separated from the man who held it, but there is undoubtedly a great difference of degree in the closeness of the relationship. With Nietzsche the union of the two has been carried to its highest possible point. He did not deliberately stand apart from his philosophy, and let his intellect give it form, without let or hindrance from the other sides of his nature. He did not attempt to remove all the subjective elements. Instead, he went to the other extreme, and made no selection at all. Everything was equally valuable, his intellectual convictions, his æsthetic tastes, his likes and dislikes. Even his whims were worthy of consideration ; sometimes it seems as if they held the place of honor. The result of all this is that his philosophy is the picture of himself. It is the expression of his own many-sided personality. One cannot separate the two : the man and his work must be considered together.

Closely related to the personal character of Nietzsche's philosophy, is the individual nature of the value ascribed to all theories and opinions. Many are ready to admit, with Fichte, that the philosophy which a man chooses, depends upon the kind of a man he is. Not so easy of acceptance is the corollary, that since every other person is a different man, his thinking will differ from

---

[1] Cf. Alois Riehl (*Friedrich Nietzsche. Der Künstler und der Denker*, p. 55), who says that the problem of culture binds together the different periods.

one's own, but need not on that account be any less valuable. Nietzsche not only accepted both statements, but rather placed the emphasis upon the second. He denied that there were any absolute standards of measurement. Truth is always my truth and your truth; it cannot exist apart from us. Moreover, any consensus of opinion with regard to an idea detracts from its value. You insult me by daring to agree with me, you men of smaller calibre; you have pulled my truth down to a lower plane; it has no longer any worth for me.

This aristocratic tendency is one of the most strongly marked characteristics of Nietzsche's work. It is not intended for the crowd. What have they to do with philosophy? It is strictly for the nobility; for those with the finer perceptions and delicate discrimination of the gentleman. It knows nothing of the common people, and wishes to know nothing: they have no significance for the patrician. Nietsche's opinions upon special subjects are often the result of this attitude. A certain theory of morals must be rejected, because it savors too much of the vulgar. Some view of life under discussion is held worthy of consideration: it pays due regard to the little niceties of social intercourse. This, that, and the other opinion are looked at and found wanting from the half instinctive feeling that they are not fitting for the " Count Niëtzky."

Nietzsche's style has been much praised by friends and enemies alike. In this respect, as well as in others, he is often compared to Schopenhauer. Indeed, he expresses himself so clearly and directly, that he often seems to approach the great French masters of style, whom he admired so much, and perhaps took as his model. One may hesitate to call him the greatest writer of the age, as some of his followers do; but there is enough praise for him, even if one does not go beyond the more moderate of his critics. Riehl,[1] for instance, says that Nietzsche has widened the capacity for expression of the German language, and enriched the German literature with a few masterpieces of sentences. Elsewhere the same author warns us not to take Nietzsche too literally, for he was an artist, and loved the forms

---

[1] *Friedrich Nietsche. Der Künstler und der Denker.* p. 131.

of speech, the color of the words, the strength of the expression. "All his artistic instincts are united in his style. His relation to speech is that of the poet, musician, and painter." [1]

One of the great difficulties in the study of Nietzsche's philosophy is the frequent change of standpoint that it underwent.[2] Nietzsche was like Schelling in that he carried on his philosophical education in public. The whole process of development, even in its most minute stages, is displayed to view. The consequence is that, when one desires to explain Nietzsche's opinion with regard to a certain question, it is always necessary to state the period at which he held it. The exposition of a philosophy under a dozen or twenty different aspects is manifestly impossible. The best one can do is to take certain broad divisions, and ignore the slighter changes. As a matter of fact, Nietzsche's writings lend themselves readily to a triple division. The first, which may be called the æsthetic period, embraces the *Geburt der Tragödie* und *Unzeitgemässe Betrachtungen.* To the second, the intellectual period, belong the two volumes of *Menschliches allzu Menschliches. Morgenröte* and *Die fröhliche Wissenschaft* form a transition stage, and contain characteristics belonging both to the preceding period and to the ethical and final one. This latter contains the rest of Nietzsche's published works, namely, *Also sprach Zarathustra, Jenseits von Gut und Böse, Zur Geneologie der Moral, Der Fall Wagner, Nietzsche contra Wagner, Götzendämmerung,* and *Antichrist.* Such a classification is followed by practically all [3] the commentators on Neitzsche, with the exception

[1] *Op. cit.,* p. 31.

[2] Rudolf Steiner in *Friedrich Nietzsche. Ein Kämpfer gegen seine Zeit,* p. 96, says that the early books express the same thoughts as the later, but concealed in Schopenhaurian and Wagnerian forms.

[3] *E. g.,* A. Seth Pringle Pattison in *Blackwood's Magazine* for Oct., '97, p. 487, and Waldmann : *Friedrich Nietzsche. Ein Blick in Seine Werke vom Standpunkte eines Laien,* pp. 1–10, and others, including E. v. Hartmann, *Ethische Studien,* p. 36. Some writers make a twofold division, *e. g.,* Fuchs (*Friedrich Nietzsche. Sein Leben und Seine Lehre mit besonderer Berücksichtigung seiner Stellung zum Christentum,* p. 35) places in the second period all the works later than *Unzeitgemässe Betrachtungen.* In some instances, the divisions, though chronologically the same as those mentioned above, are given different names. *E. g.,* Frau Lou Andreas-Salomé (*Friedrich Nietzsche in seinen Werken,* p. 10) calls the first period that of Schopenhauer's influence, while Hannson (*Friedrich Neitzsche, seine Persönlichkeit und sein System,* p. 131) makes a twofold division, the second period of which begins with the rupture of the friendship with Wagner.

that some of them place *Morgenröte* and *Die fröhliche Wissenschaft*
in the second period, instead of regarding them as belonging
equally to this and to the third.   There are various opinions with
regard to relationship of the three periods to one another.   Most
writers [1] seem to regard the second as having little connection
with the first and third, which in their turn are looked upon as
closely united.   On the other hand, it is perfectly possible to regard the third period as the natural development of the second,
and to find the sudden break rather in the transition from the
first to the second.   The decision depends almost entirely upon
the unifying principle that one chooses.   The controlling motive
of Nietzsche was never a theory, but something much more indefinite.   It seems sometimes as if his whole philosophy were
in answer to the question concerning the ultimate good.   If life
is worth living, what is it that makes it so?   What is the su-
premely valuable?   During the first period, he approached this
question from the æsthetic point of view, and he gave it the
answer of an artist.   The justification of the world, if it has one,
the reason for its existence, is the purely æsthetic concept—
beauty.   To be sure, he does not always state the matter so
simply as this.   Perhaps he was not very clear about it in his
own mind, but he certainly subjected everything to this one
canon, and accepted everything that accorded with it.   The
special problems that he discussed were all approached, and
even chosen from this point of view.   Questions as to truth,
morality, and the like did not interest him.   He was concerned
only with art, taking the word in its broadest sense.   Between
this period and the next there is seemingly a complete break
in thought, because his standard of valuation had changed.
Truth had become the one desirable thing for him.   Naturally,
then, he no longer discussed such questions as the origin of Greek
tragedy, but devoted himself to a criticism of the concepts of true
and false, as they are usually held.   He questioned the validity
of religion and morality, as well as of logic.   He devoted much
time to what he called psychology; that is, a minute examination
of the peculiarities of human character, especially their motives

[1] A. Seth Pringle Pattison, *Op. cit.*, p. 487.

and their origin.   He interested himself in almost every conceivable topic relating to culture, but everything was judged in accordance with the same intellectual standard.   The third period is really the logical outcome of the second.   He saw that once having begun to question the standards of value, there was no reason why he should stop at any particular point.   Hitherto he had doubted the validity of truth as commonly accepted ; now he set aside the concept of truth itself.   His individualism had been carried to an extreme.   The only valuation left him, after the rejection of the æsthetic and intellectual standpoints, seems to be almost of an ethical nature.   As will be seen later, everything is of value that can further the development of the Overman.   Whatever does not promote this end, whether it is true or false, good or bad, beautiful or ugly, is to be rigorously cast aside. Many of the topics discussed in the second period are again considered, but the conclusion reached is, in many cases, necessarily different.   A new standard of value has been set up, and the world has therefore a different aspect.

Even apart, however, from these chronological changes, there are many inconsistencies and contradictions in Nietzsche's writings, and a connected interpretation is correspondingly difficult. In fact, his choice of subjects and the method of their treatment was determined by two mental tendencies, in themselves antagonistic, namely, artistic feeling and critical keenness.[1]   Sometimes one gained the upper hand, sometimes the other, but neither ever entirely disappeared.   His æsthetic sensibility prompted him to trust his instincts, to feel rather than to think, to regard the world as a unity, a harmony.   At the same time, however, the merciless faculty of analysis and criticism drove him to reject much that the artist found good, to break down instead of building up, to regard nothing as sacred, least of all his own convictions.   The conflict between these two warring elements, already apparent in his first book, the *Geburt der Tragödie*, continues all through the later publications ; and

---

[1] Lichtenberger (*Aphorismes et Fragments choisis*, pref., pp. vi, vii) says that Nietzsche's work shows two tendencies, one affirmative, the other negative. The first, which predominated at the beginning of his career, led him to enthusiasm, the second to criticism.

even in the last one of all it is still present. The union of this ill-assorted pair accounts for the way in which Nietzsche is now called a mystic, now a positivist. Logically the two epithets may be mutually exclusive, but with respect to a writer like Nietzsche they are both true. A human mind is not a series of syllogisms, and opinions must often be inconsistent, if more than one mental tendency is to be satisfied.

During the first period, the æsthetic impulse was in predominance. Nietzsche's great desire was to find some point of view that would permit him to regard the world and human life as an artistic whole. The critical faculty, if not in abeyance, filled at least a strictly subordinate position. It had led him to discard all religious faith, but he did not yet display any especial interest in his own denials. He simply did not discuss the subject. The positive aspect had more attraction for him. In the same way, although he could not accept many of the current theories in æsthetics, he dwelt rather upon the constructive side of his own views and not upon their critical basis.

Afterward he began to devote himself to criticism for its own sake. During the intellectual period, which is that containing the greatest number of contradictions, the two tendencies appear side by side. Æsthetics, however, though still occupying an important place, is no longer supreme. As has already been mentioned, the standard of value has become intellectual, and the one question of absorbing interest is that concerning the nature of truth. Instead of the attempt to find harmony and artistic purpose everywhere, the most striking feature of the books written at this period is their keen and often destructive analysis. At the third and final stage of Nietzsche's development, contradictory as it may seem, both tendencies appear to have gained strength. Criticism has been carried to its utmost lengths; and on the other hand, artistic harmony often puts aside all critical analysis. A more detailed statement of the influence of these two forces is impossible, until after a consideration of the theories themselves.

CHAPTER II.

The Æsthetic Period.

Sec. 1. General Characteristics.

Until the publication of *Die Geburt der Tragödie* in December, 1871, Nietzsche's literary activity was entirely of a philological[1] nature. He investigated questions concerning Diogenes Laertius and Theognis, while his article upon the strife between Homer and Hesiod is of sufficient importance to be quoted in Mahaffy's *History of Classical Greek Literature*.[2] That he did some philosophical work at the same time is shown by the papers[3] that have been collected and published since his final break-down; but these are all brief and fragmentary, and seem to be the reflection of his reading, rather than the result of independent thought. During his university years he devoted himself almost entirely to the study of philology; and for a long time afterward the course of his thinking was naturally determined by this preparation. Everything was subordinated to the one intellectual interest. Even his passion for Schopenhauer was no exception. Schopenhauer was always more a prophet than a philosopher to him; and when he accepted the chair of philology at Bâle, it was with the intention of infusing the Schopenhauerian life into the dry bones of philology. With re-

---

[1] Frau Lou Andreas-Salomé (*Friedrich Nietzsche in seinen Werken*, p. 51) gives the following list of Nietzsche's philological publications: *Zur Geschichte der Theognideischen Sprachsammlung*, in the *Rheinisches Museum*, Bd. 22; *Beiträge zur Kritik der griechischen Lyriker, I. Der Danae Klage von Simonides*, in *Rhein. Mus.*, Bd. 23; *De Laertii Diogeni Fontibus*, in *Rhein. Mus.*, Bd. 23 and 24; *Analecta Laertiana*, in *Rhein. Mus.*, Bd. 25; *Beiträge zur Quellen-Kunde und Kritik des Laertius Diogenes, Gratulationsscrift des Pädagogiums zu Basel. Basel*, 1870; *Certamen quod dicitur Homeri et Hesiode e codice Florentino post H. Stephanum denno ed. Friedrich Nietzsche*, in the *Acta societatis philologae Lipsiensis ed.* Fr. Ritschl, vol. I; *Der florentinische Tractat über Homer und Hesiod, ihr Geschlecht und ihren Wettkampf*. in *Rhein. Mus.*, Bd. 25 and 28. Also the index to the first 24 volumes of the *Rheinisches Museum* (1842–1869).

[2] Vol. I, pp. 118, 119.

[3] *Das Leben Friedrich Nietzsche's*, I, *Anhang; Werke*, IX.

[4] *Ibid.*, I, 306.

gard to the subject in general his dream came to little.   Philology
and philologians continued to pursue the even tenor of their
way, without much notice of Schopenhauer or his disciple.   The
dry bones refused to come to life.   Nietzsche succeeded better,
however, with his own work.   It certainly became Schopenhauerian, although at the same time, it grew less and less philological.   The field remained the same, but the method changed.
The emphasis had shifted, and much that Nietzsche called
philology, seems to be rather æsthetics or the history of various
ideas.   It was all preëminently the work of a man who had been
a philologian, but was one no longer.   The precision, the respect
for the individual word, remained ; the subjects chosen were
those with which his previous work had made him familiar ; but
a new spirit had come into the work, and philosophy was rapidly
gaining the upper hand.   For a long time the influence of philology was still apparent, but it grew less and less, and finally almost entirely disappeared.

During the whole of this early period Nietzsche's chief interest
lay in æsthetics, and his general attitude was that of the man
who places art and culture before everything else.   It is perhaps
harder for the English-speaking race than for any other to com-
prehend the artistic temperament.   Not only have the Anglo-
Saxons a keen eye for practical advantages, but even their
ideals are to a large extent non-æsthetic.   They can understand an intellectual point of view.   Nearly every educated man
among the English-speaking peoples has an inborn respect for the
fact, and a still deeper reverence for any scheme of the world
that coördinates the facts, and reduces them to a system.   The
ardor of the scientist is not at all an unknown quantity.   The
emphasis that he puts upon truth, and the sacrifices that he makes
for it, are familiar.   He measures everything by the one standard,
and nothing that does not promise to increase knowledge and to
help to establish truth is worthy, according to him, of much consideration.

Much greater emphasis, however, is laid upon the moral values.
The universe is a moral universe.   With the rejection of morality,
life would seem to lose all meaning, all worth.   We may put aside

religious creeds ; we may cease to believe in another and better world, which supplies the *raison d'être* for this present existence ; we may lose all remembrance of the God of our fathers ; but good and evil retain all their former force. The moral law is still the ultimate, beyond which we cannot go. Its content may be changed ; it may be regarded as the result of long development under purely natural conditions ; but it continues to be the moral law, and never loses its imperative character. Everything else is subjected to its criterion. Immoral art is thrust aside, denied the very name of art. Unless there is a moral order of the world, all its problems are hopelessly insoluble ; nothing else can give an aim to life, make it at all worth the living, justify its terrible tragedy. Without morality, everything is a dreary chaos ; there is no law and order anywhere. It is useless to fall back upon the old maxim : " Eat, drink, and be merry, for to-morrow ye die," for the satisfaction is gone even from the more sensual pleasures. In every attempt to picture such a condition there is always some vestige of morality to be found about the edges, just as empty space always has some boundary.

For the artistic standpoint all this is changed. Moral and intellectual values cease to be the only ones, and even become subordinate to others. Beauty is the supreme reason for existence. The intellectual or moral life is no longer the only possibility. It is on a lower plane than the artistic life, where the law of beauty is recognized. In fact, the chief virtue left to morality is its æsthetic side. There is no necessity for a moral basis of the universe, which will do quite as well without it. Life is not a series of problems to be solved ; neither is it a task to be accomplished. If the world is beautiful, why need we look further ? Any amount of toil and hardship is justified, if it produces only a little music, or painting, or poetry. One song compensates for all the tragedy of existence. One does not ask whether a book has a moral or immoral tendency. The only relevant question is : May it be classed as a work of art ? Otherwise it deserves no consideration.

This whole point of view is often incomprehensible to the man to whom truth and goodness seem fundamental, but it was

Nietzsche's standpoint during the early period of his literary activity, and his theories can be understood only when this fact is continually kept in mind.   For instance, he makes the artist the end and aim of the world ; he regards the birth of tragedy as the most important moment in Greek history ; he professes almost complete agreement with Schopenhauer's æsthetic theories, and gives to Wagner, the musician, the supreme place in his dreams of the culture of the future.   For him, the ultimate questions are not moral, but artistic.   It is not only art for art's sake, but life for art's sake.[1]

All of Nietzsche's particular opinions must be judged in the light of this general standpoint, for they were determined by it. With many thinkers, the special theories are much more important than the point of view.   They are not only valuable in themselves, but they furnish the clue to the system as a whole.   With Nietzsche, all this is reversed.   His general standpoint is not only of more interest and value than his opinions upon various subjects, but it also furnishes their best commentary and explanation.   The point of view is the expression of the kind of man he was, and the particular theories are intimately related to the point of view.   The latter can be understood almost alone ; the former are meaningless, when taken from their setting.   As has already been pointed out, in this early period, with its essentially æsthetic character, the influence of the critical tendency is not so apparent as it later becomes.   So far as concerns the books published at this time, its effect is negative rather than positive. Nietzsche had long been a sceptic in religion, but here his position on this point is indicated more by omissions than by definite statements.   Intellectual doubts had not become sufficiently imperative to outweigh the artist's desire for a harmony that knows no question but simply accepts what it finds.

Before entering upon the discussion of Nietzsche's æsthetic period, to which belong the two books, *Die Geburt der Tragödie* and *Unzeitgemässe Betrachtungen*, it must be premised that the chronological divisions are not to be taken too strictly. Nietzsche never ceased to feel an interest in the questions of art,

[1] *Die Geburt der Tragödie, Werke,* I, p. 8.

and continued to discuss them, with more or less minuteness, until his illness put an end to all intellectual work. All that can be done is to select the predominant characteristics of each successive period, with the understanding that they are not mutually exclusive. Thus, much could be written with regard to his views upon art during what have been called the intellectual and ethical periods, but for the sake of convenience they have been included in the present chapter. When his standpoint remained the same, references to the later books have been omitted, but all changes have, of course, been duly noted.

Sec. 2. Theories of Art and Culture.

Among the fragments published in the last four volumes of the Naumann edition of Nietzsche's works, those written at this early period contain a fragmentary statement of a theory of the ultimate nature of the universe. Although in general no attention will be paid to the volumes in question, inasmuch as they are composed of matter that Nietzsche rejected at the time when he was preparing his manuscripts for the press; yet, in this case, they are merely the expression of what is constantly implied in *Die Geburt der Tragödie,* and so will be discussed in brief. Nietzsche began life, philosophically speaking, as a follower of Schopenhauer,[1] so it is a matter of course that he should regard the will as the ultimate. It is the *Ding an sich,* and the intellect is purely phenomenal in character.[2] Nothing exists, save the will and its manifestations. In its efforts to attain individuality, it gives rise to the phenomenal world, including man. Yet all the varied forms which it assumes are less than nothing in themselves. Their only value to the will lies in the degree in which they

---

[1] *Werke,* IX, p. 47.

[2] Later Nietzsche came to regard the influence of Schopenhauer as unimportant, and to see in his own book, *Die Geburt der Tragödie,* only Schopenhauer's forms without his content. Unfortunately for the value of this self-estimate, Nietzsche was prone to look upon any change in his opinion of some other writer, as a proof of former lack of comprehension. As his own views took more definite shape, he liked to explain his separation from some former master, by saying that he had read his own ideas into the other, and saw now that there had never been any agreement between them. A detailed treatment of the relation between the two may be conveniently postponed, until after a discussion of the other portions of Nietzsche's system.

further existence.[1] The will affirms everything that gives as-
surance of permanence, whether it be art, morality, religion, what
you will.

Instinct, the expression of the will, obliges man to act, and
the world of idea is merely the motive for action.[2] It seems to
be more real than the will, but is therein deceptive. Nevertheless,[3]
upon it rests all individuation. This does not mean that the
world of individuals depends upon each and every human brain.
The idea is not to be regarded so anthropomorphically. Rather,
individuation is the work of the original intellect, which reveals
itself in conscious intellects, only in so far as they are instinct.

For Nietzsche in this early stage, as well as for Schopenhauer,
pessimism was a necessary assumption. With the former, however, it did not lead to quietism. He denied that the essence of
art and of morality lay altogether in the negation of the individual,
although, as will be seen, there are traces of the Schopenhauerian
view. Pessimism should lead to action, and it may be a sign of
vitality. For Nietzsche these terms are synonymous with artistic
creation and vitality of art. In fact, the question of the nature
of pessimism interested him only upon its æsthetic side, and his
examination of it took the form of a discussion of Greek tragedy,
in which he endeavored to discover the elements of its greatness
and the cause of its decline. This involved a consideration of
the ultimate nature of art, and of the tendencies of ancient and
modern culture. As he himself stated the problem in 1886, the
question was : "Is pessimism necessarily a sign of degeneration,
as it was with the East Indians, and probably is with the modern
Europeans ? Is there a pessimism of strength, perhaps a suffering caused by over-supply, a courage that demands a worthy
enemy against which it can prove its strength ? "[4] Socratic dialectic killed Greek tragedy. Perhaps the cheerfulness of the
theoretical man is a sign of degeneration, and science is only a
flight from pessimism.

The whole discussion presupposes that the Greeks of the tragic
age were pessimists, an assumption, which, as Riehl says, is

[1] *Werke*, IX, p. 47.   [3] *Ibid.*, p. 66.
[2] *Ibid.*, p. 65.   [4] *Werke*, I, pp. 2, 3.

due to one of those revelations of the Hellenic nature, vouch-safed only to Nietzsche.[1] He never sought to justify his position ; it seemed to be altogether a matter of course to him. He re-gards the development of art as bound together with the duality of the Dionysian and Apollinic tendencies,[2] an opinion which is doubtless his one important contribution to theories of æsthetics. These tendencies are typified by the two art-gods of the Greeks, Dionysus and Apollo. The realm of the latter embraces every-thing pictorial, plastic ; it is the dream world. The philosopher[3] feels that beneath the actuality in which we live, another, entirely different, lies hidden. In the same way, the artist never loses the consciousness that his dream, his picture, is only appearance (*Schein*). The very essence of the Apollinic lies in this recog-nition ; yet, at the same time,[4] there is no falsification in the ap-pearance. Apollo, the god of appearance, is also the truth-speaker, the giver of oracles. He expresses a freedom from wild impulses, a wise rest. He is like Schopenhauer's man veiled in Maia. He is the contemplative spirit,[5] the most royal picture of the *principium individuationis*. Of the two halves of life, the wáking and the dreaming, the former seems to us to be inex-pressibly the more important ;[6] but for the mysterious ground of our existence, of which we are only the phenomenon, just the reversed valuation holds good. The more one is aware of the powerful art-impulses of nature, and their longing for deliverance, the more is one forced to the metaphysical assumption that the truly beënt and original one, that is, the ultimate will, inasmuch as it is the eternally suffering and contradictory, needs the ecstatic vision, the pleasurable appearance for its continual deliverance. This appearance we are obliged to apprehend as the non-beënt,[7] that is, as a continual becoming in time, space, and causality ; in other words, as empirical reality. If empirical existence is once

---

[1] *Friedrich Nietzsche. Der Künstler und der Denker*, p. 49.
[2] *Die Geburt der Tragödie, Werke*, I, p. 19.
[3] *Ibid.*, p. 21.
[4] *Ibid.*, p. 22.
[5] *Ibid.*, p. 23.
[6] *Ibid.*, p. 34.
[7] *Ibid.*, p. 35.

understood as an idea (*Vorstellung*) of the original One, then the
dream becomes the appearance of the appearance, and thereby a
still higher satisfaction of the original impulse.   In Apollo, the
aim of the original One, its deliverance through appearance,[1] is
brought to completion.   He shows us how the whole world of
agony is necessary, in order that the individual may be compelled
to produce the delivering vision.

If Apollo is the god of dreams, Dionysus is the god of intoxication.[2]   The Dionysian tendency arises from the union of
horror at finding oneself mistaken in the knowledge of the phenomenon, with the ecstacy at the destruction of the *principium individuationis*.[3]   This manifests itself especially in music.   Sometimes it comes about through the influence of narcotic drinks,
sometimes at the approach of spring.   Through its magic, the
bond between man and man and that between man and nature, is
drawn more closely.[4]   Every one feels himself, not only united
with his neighbor, but one with him.   It is lack of all measure,
of all bounds.[5]   Man is no longer an artist, but a work of art.   In
the shudder of intoxication, there is revealed the artistic might
of nature, striving for the satisfaction of the original One.[6]

Every artist imitates one of these conditions of nature, either
the dream or the intoxication.   Sometimes, as in the Greek
tragedy, both tendencies are united.   For a long time the Dionysian found no footing in Greece,[7] and the reconciliation between it and the Apollinic is the most important moment in the
history of Greek culture.   Here Dionysian orgies first became
festivals of the world's salvation, the tearing asunder of the
principle of individuation first became an artistic phenomenon.
The Greek recognized the terribleness of life.   He needed the
dream world, the realm of Apollo, in order to live at all.   The
Dionysian element made its appearance later with the beginning
of lyric poetry.[8]   The lyric poet is entirely united with the
original One, with the will, its pain and contradiction, and produces a copy of it as music.   This music takes the visible form of

[1] *Op. cit.*, p. 36.
[2] *Ibid.*, p. 20.
[3] *Ibid.*, p. 23.
[4] *Ibid.*, p. 24.
[5] *Ibid.*, p. 37.
[6] *Ibid.*, p. 25.
[7] *Ibid.*, p. 27.
[8] *Ibid.*, p. 39.

a dream picture, and the Dionysian and Apollinic are no longer opposed. It is all an expression of the eternal necessity of nature. The whole comedy of art[1] does not exist for us, neither do we create it. For the true creator, we are artistic projections, and as such have our highest value. It is only as æsthetic phenomenon that the world is eternally justified. Our very knowledge of art is illusory, for in so far as we are knowing beings, we cease to be one with the creator. Only the genius who, in the act of artistic creation, is completely united with the original artist of the world, knows something about the nature of art.

It is not necessary to discuss in detail Nietzsche's theory of the origin of Greek tragedy. In the Dionysian element, he thinks he sees the essence of the spirit of music; and in his account of the Greek chorus and other related subjects he endeavors to show that tragedy begins with its introduction. Only when we start with the spirit of music can we understand the pleasure in the destruction of the individual, which tragedy affords us. The hero, the highest phenomenon of the will, is denied, because he is only phenomenon, and the eternal life of the will is not thereby disturbed. It must be admitted that Nietzsche's arguments are not always convincing, at least to those readers who have not been blessed with the Hellenic revelations, of which Riehl speaks.

With the advent of Euripides[2] a new element appeared, which finally destroyed tragedy. This was the Socratic spirit, which recognized as the highest law, that, to be beautiful, everything must be comprehensible. Here philosophic thought outgrew art, and forced it into a close relationship with dialectic, which is essentially optimistic.[3] The death of tragedy lies in the three fundamental forms of optimism: (1) Virtue is knowledge; (2) One sins only through ignorance; and (3) The virtuous is the happy. Socrates is the type[4] of the theoretic optimist, who supposes[5] that thought reaches to the very depths of being, and who ascribes to knowledge the value of a universal medicine. He was

---

[1] *Op. cit.*, pp. 44, 45.
[2] *Ibid.*, pp. 86, 92.
[3] *Ibid.*, p. 100.
[4] *Ibid.*, p. 107.
[5] *Ibid.*, p. 105.

the first to live and die for science, and so was the turning point in the history of the world.

There is a contradiction, then, between mere learning, even of the most exact and scientific kind, and a true culture. The one indispensable characteristic of the latter is vitality.[1] It is fulness of life. The problem of culture is almost identical with that of philosophy, for, as Nietzsche says over and over again, philosophy is of no value, unless it concerns itself with life instead of with abstractions. As he himself states the question : "What is the problem of culture? To live and to work in the noblest strivings of one's nation and of humanity. Not only, therefore, to receive and to learn, but to live. To free one's age and people from wrong tendencies, to have one's ideal before one's eyes."[2] "The problem of the cultivated man is to be truthful and to put himself actually in relationship to everything great. Culture is life in the meaning of great spirits, with the aim of great ends." It is vitality that makes the Greek culture of the tragic age deep in significance, and it is lack of vitality that marks the decline following upon the appearance of Euripides and Socrates.

With the exception of philosophy and music,[3] modern culture is essentially Socratic. Optimism is supreme. The men of to-day are learned, but not cultured in the true sense. One of the dangers threatening them arises from the excessive attention now devoted to all departments of historical study. The man who cannot forget, i. e., think unhistorically, will never know happiness himself, nor do anything to make others know it.[4] His personality is weakened.[5] History is spoiled by the demand that it be scientific. Facts, without the ability to digest them, are worth nothing.[6] We modern men get nothing out of ourselves; we are mere encyclopædias of information about other times. We forget that culture is something alive,

<hr />

[1] *Vom Nutzen und Nachtheil der Historie für das Leben*, *Werke*, I, pp. 314, 378.

[2] *Das Leben Friedrich Nietzs.he's*, II, p. iii.

[3] *Die Geburt der Tragödie*, *Werke*, I, pp. 125, 127, 138.

[4] *Unzeitgemässe Betrachtungen* ; *Vom Nutzen und Nachtheil der Historie für das Leben*, I, p. 285.

[5] *Ibid.*, p. 319.

[6] *Ibid.*, p. 311.

and make it a knowledge about culture.[1] History is useful only when it is subservient to life.

Much more inexcusable than excess of historical study is the smug self-satisfaction that regards the present condition of affairs as the only desirable one. The severest criticism of this contentment is found in *David Strauss, der Bekenner und der Schriftsteller.* This essay is a polemic against the 'philistine of culture,' an expression of Nietzsche's own coinage, upon which he prided himself. Strauss was held up to ridicule as the representative of a class. At the close of the Franco-German war, there was a wide-spread opinion that the victory of the German arms meant also the victory of German culture. As if the Germans had any culture to be victorious![2] "Culture is above all the unity of artistic style in all the manifestations of the life of a people";[3] and it is this essential unity that Germany lacks. The worst of the matter is, that Germans are so profoundly oblivious of their shortcomings. Even the learned classes join in the sleek self-satisfaction that marks philistinism.[4] They suppose that art is only for leisure moments, and must not be allowed to interfere with the serious business of life. There are two characteristics that distinguish German culture: (1) It is profoundly self-satisfied, and consequently unwilling for any changes, and as a natural result, believes most devoutly in the peculiar value of the German educational system. (2) It places the highest judgment upon all questions of art and taste in the hands of the learned, and regards itself as an ever-growing compendium of learned opinions upon art, literature, and philosophy.[5] It never sees that learning and culture do not necessarily go together, that knowledge is neither an indispensable means of culture, nor a sign of it.[6]

The mere absence of faults, however, does not constitute culture. For that a positive element is necessary, and nowhere more so than in education. Every soul must learn to stand alone, to live its own life, undisturbed by the accidents of climate,

---

[1] *Op. cit.*, p. 314.
[2] *Ibid.*, p. 179.
[3] *Ibid.*, p. 183.
[4] *Ibid.*, pp. 185, 190.
[5] *Ibid.*, p. 233.
[6] *Ibid.*, p. 183.

nation, surrounding opinions, and religions.[1] The only true edu-
cator is he who teaches this freedom, and for Nietzsche the term
is practically synonymous with the name of Schopenhauer. In
his works are to be found the characteristics of a true culture;
he not only tells us what it is, but he points out the way by
which it is to be attained. "I belong to the readers of Schopenhauer," Nietzsche writes, "who, after they have read the first
page of him know with certainty that they will read all his pages,
and will listen to every word that he has said. My trust in him
was at once present, and is now the same that it was nine years
ago. I understood him as if he had written for me, to make use
of a comprehensible but vain and foolish expression. Thence it
comes that I have never found in him a paradox, although here
and there a small error; for what are paradoxes but observations
that inspire no confidence, because the author made them with
no real confidence himself, because he wished to shine with them,
to mislead, and to make a show? Schopenhauer never wishes
to make a show; for he writes for himself, and no one desires to
be deceived, least of all a philosopher who takes as his law: De-
ceive no one, not even thyself! Not even with the pleasant
social deception, which almost every conversation brings with it,
and which writers almost unconsciously imitate; still less with
the more conscious deception of the lecture platform and with
the ingenious means of rhetoric. But Schopenhauer talks to
himself; or, if one must think of a listener, then think of the
son whom his father is teaching."[2] Schopenhauer is honorable,
even as an author. Montaigne alone stands higher than he in
this respect. The two have another trait in common, also,
namely, cheerfulness of the true sort, not the undignified kind
that makes grimaces, and sees no suffering at all. The union
of this honorableness and cheerfulness with reliability compose
the physiological impression, so to speak, that Schopenhauer
makes, the magic outflow of power from one growth of nature
to another, as soon as they come in contact.

A philosopher is to be valued only to the degree that he can

[1] *Schopenhauer als Erzieher, Werke,* I, pp. 386–392.
[2] *Ibid.,* p. 398.

give an example through his visible life and not merely through books. Kant held fast to the university, was subject to the governments, maintained the semblance of a religious belief among colleagues and students; and it is natural that his example should produce university professors and a professorial philosophy. Schopenhauer separated himself from all this, and is a living example of the fact that philosophy should not be pure science.[1] He teaches us to distinguish between the real and apparent demands of human happiness, and shows us that striving for good things gains worth only through a common aim.[2]

At the present state of culture, the one thing most needful is the picture of a real man. Three such have been given to the world, that of Rousseau, that of Goethe, and that of Schopenhauer.[3] The last-named is, on the whole, the most admirable. The Schopenhauerian man takes upon himself the voluntary suffering that comes from truthfulness, from refusing to accept what he does not honestly believe; and this helps him to destroy his own will, and to bring about the complete change in his nature, the accomplishment of which gives life its true meaning. This truth-speaking often seems to other men like wickedness. In reality, there is a denial and destruction that is the result of a mighty longing for holiness and rescue. All existence that can be denied, deserves to be denied.

The Schopenhauerian man destroys his own happiness through his courage. He is hostile to men and institutions that he loves, and therefore is misunderstood. He realizes, however, that a happy life is impossible, and that the highest that a man can attain is a heroic life. So long as one demands life as happiness, one has not yet raised one's eyes beyond the horizon of the animal. Those who help to bring about such insight are the true men, the philosophers, artists, and saints. They discover a new circle of duties through which they are not separated from the community, but rather bound together with it in the fundamental thought of a culture and a task that are common to all. This latter is the

[1] *Op. cit.*, p. 403.
[2] *Ibid.*, p. 411.
[3] *Ibid.*, p. 424.

production of the philosopher, the artist, and the saint, both in ourselves and in others. The feeling that we can do nothing toward this end is the root of Schopenhauer's pessimism, which is the beginning, not the end of his philosophy. We must learn to hate something besides ourselves. This is the first consecration of culture. The second comes when one seeks in the world what one has already found in oneself. The last and final step is the fight for culture, the hostility to all forces that do not make for the production of genius.[1]

In our times, the philosophical genius can arise only under the following conditions: free manliness of character, early knowledge of men, no learned education, no patriotic narrowness, no compulsion toward winning a livelihood, no relations to governments—in short, complete freedom.[2] These were the conditions under which Schopenhauer lived; and his philosophy will bear the only criticism that is worth anything, namely, one can live according to it.

In Wagner, Nietzsche thought he had found a living example of the Schopenhauerian man as artist,[3] one who fulfilled all the conditions, who dared to live his own life—more than that, to create his own art. The prophecy, in *Die Geburt der Tragödie*, of the modern reawakening[4] of Greek tragedy in the union of the Apollinic and Dionysian forces is an unmistakeable description of the Wagnerian opera. After the break with Wagner, Nietzsche regarded this as an error, and found the distinctive characteristic of Wagner's music to be not Greek, but romantic.[5] Error or truth, however, at this time Wagner stood for the incarnation of his ideal, as the artistic expression, so to speak, of his own theories. He says that there are two impulses in Wagner's nature, the strong will, which demands force, and the impulse toward truth.[6] Wagner simplified the world, in that he found a relation between music and life, and music and the drama.

[1] *Op. cit.*, pp. 425–445.
[2] *Ibid.*, p. 474.
[3] *Richard Wagner in Bayreuth, Werke*, I, *passim.*
[4] *Die Geburt der Tragödie, Werke*, I, pp. 143–169.
[5] *Ibid.*, p. 7, preface, written in 1886.
[6] *Richard Wagner in Bayreuth*, pp. 504–506.

He asked himself the question : What is the significance of the fact that in modern life such an art as music has come to have such strength ? He found that music, in its protest against artificial estrangement, is a return to nature. Moreover, the relation between music and life expresses that between the complete world of hearing and the complete world of vision. Modern life is poor in the latter. In Wagner everything visible deepens itself into the audible, and everything audible deepens itself into the visible. He gives a language to that part of nature that has hitherto been silent. If the philosopher says that there is one will in nature, which thirsts for existence, the musician adds that the existence thus willed is audible.[1]

[1] *Op. cit.*, pp. 524, 567.

CHAPTER III.

THE INTELLECTUAL PERIOD.

The publication of *Menschliches allzu Menschliches*, which followed closely the last of the *Unzeitgemässe Betrachtungen*, marks a different phase of Nietzsche's development. During the first period, as has been shown, he was concerned with questions closely related to æsthetics ; and if he did occasionally discuss other topics, it was always from the artistic point of view. Now all that is changed. Suddenly the question of absorbing interest becomes the epistemological one of the nature of truth and of man's relation to it: Nietzsche the artist has become Nietzsche the philosopher. He is still the opponent of the greater part of the existing culture, and still the prophet of something better to be striven for in the future ; but now he preaches salvation through the intellect, not through the artistic instincts. The man of science has a more exalted position than the artist. This change is the direct result of the greater importance given to methods of criticism. Instead of regarding the world as a whole, an artistic projection, as he says, Nietzsche had begun to ask questions about the parts that make up the whole. He was no longer satisfied with the contemplation of æsthetic beauty, and had taken another step in the direction of that destructive criticism, which was one day to hail him among its most radical defenders.

It is a natural result of this different standpoint, that the subjects treated are not the same as those discussed in the earlier books. Besides the epistemological question *per se*, there are others, which are more or less akin to it, and which seem for the first time to have awakened Nietzsche's attention. When the critical interest had once gained the upper hand, everything came to be subjected to searching analysis. Problems in ethics, in religion, in the affairs of everyday life, all were examined in order to determine (1) what we really know about them, and (2) how

34

the prevailing but false opinion gained credence. Nothing is accepted, everything must be proven. The one assumption that he deliberately makes concerns the value of truth and of the life of culture built upon it. These alone justify themselves.

Sec. 1. Truth.

What is truth, then ? Nietzsche's answer to this question is indefinite, and not very clearly stated. It can hardly be an agreement with the reality of things, because there are no things, and reality itself is doubtful. Neither can it be that which agrees with the normal functioning of the human mind, nor that which is built upon the premises of logic ; for the human mind and its logic are mistaken, both in their assumptions and in their methods. Nietzsche tells us everything that truth is not, but makes no attempt at any positive definition, although he constantly implies that there is an objective standard somewhere, and that the word ' true ' has a definite significance, which expresses the highest valuation known to us.

It is difficult to reconcile the position given to truth with Nietzsche's passionate cult of life ; for he says that all the intellectual errors further life. In fact, truth is not only an enemy to existence, but directly hostile to the development of the human reason. Error furthers happiness, and is an absolute necessity for the preservation of the race. The illogical is necessary for man.[1] It is rooted so firmly in the passions, in language, art, and religion, in everything, in fact, that lends value to life, that its destruction means the irremediable injury of the best that we know. If human nature could be changed even into an approximation of the purely logical, the loss would be incalculable. Even the most reasonable man is obliged continually to go back to the old illogical position with regard to everything. It is the price he pays for life. All his valuations, all his judgments are based upon error.[2] He supposes that deep thought, tender feelings, a high regard for himself, all bring him nearer the truth of things, and a knowledge of the actual essence of the world. Re-

[1] *Menschliches allzu Menschliches, Werke,* II, p. 48.
[2] *Ibid.,* II, pp. 21, 31, 47 ; III, pp. 24–26.

ligion and art are at bottom error, and it is error that has made man deep and sensitive enough to produce them. Not the world as thing-in-itself, but as idea, that is, as error, is of value and significance. The reason why man prefers truth to falsehood, is that, during the countless ages of his development, truth, just like the good, has been associated with the useful. He has learned that it is dangerous to make mistakes with regard to the nature of things. It was seen to be impossible to build up a reputation for oneself, and so to enjoy the approval of one's fellows, unless one really was what one seemed to be. Besides, man's self-consciousness, his ego, makes his own work seem no less important than the world, and therefore it must be as permanent. His demand for truth contains in it the belief in personal immortality. In this way, the habit arose of identifying the two concepts of the true and the productive of happiness; and the same method of reasoning was extended to all the subject matter of thought. An opinion has a good effect; therefore, it is itself good and true. It frightens and injures; therefore, it is false.[1] The effect receives the predicate good or bad, in the sense of useful or injurious, and the same predicate is then applied to the cause, in the sense of the logically good or bad. What has helped to preserve the race, and has given it all the characteristic traits that distinguish man from the other animals, what has beautified life and made it seem worth the living—all this, we are apt to think, must be true.

It is hard to admit that what has been so ardently defended in the past can be false. To die for an opinion seems almost to give evidence of its truth. In common justice it must be at least a stage of the truth. But, alas! there is no justice. Moral action has no necessary connection with intellectual insight. Probably no one ever really sacrificed himself for the truth. He wished to prove his point, because it was necessary for him to do so; the will, not the intellect, took the lead.[2] The age of convictions is that of theoretical innocence, of a belief in the possession of unconditioned truth. This presupposes that there are un-

---

[1] *Op. cit.*, II, pp. 48, 168; III, p. 29.
[2] *Ibid.*, II, pp. 75, 405.

conditioned truths, that there are perfect methods of attaining them, and, finally, that the man with a conviction has made use of the perfect methods. What nonsense !

Another inference, closely related to this one and quite as erroneous, is that whatever exists, has a right to do so is justified in fact.[1] Both conclusions go back to the fundamental error that man and the world are logical, that the objects of our love and hate, the ends that we set before ourselves, the ideals of thought and feeling which make the glory of humanity, have a basis somewhere in the fundamental essence of the world. No assumption could be more gratuitous.[2] "There is no preëstablished harmony between the furtherance of truth and the welfare of mankind." All these valuations can be traced back to their utilitarian beginning. They have no justification other than that found in their furtherance of human life. That is the standard by which they are unconsciously measured, and even the standard is the result of a similar development. All judgments about the value of life are at basis illogical, and on that account unjust.[3] The injustice is a necessity which cannot be avoided. The judgment is logically incorrect in three ways : (1) the material is incomplete ; (2) it is put together illogically ; (3) the individual parts of the material are, in their turn, the result of equally impure knowledge and methods of procedure. We cannot know enough about anything to judge it properly. Even the measure that we use, our own nature, is not a fixed quantity, but is constantly changing, and a permanent relationship to anything else is an impossibility. It would seem that the only refuge from the difficulty would be to refrain altogether from judging. Unfortunately, however, we cannot live without making valuations, without feeling attractions and repulsions. The two go together ; for there is no such thing as an impulse to or from something without an accompanying valuation, without a conviction that one is willing the useful or avoiding the harmful ; and certainly life is impossible without impulses. We are illogical beings, and we can

---

[1] *Op. cit.*, II, p. 47.

[2] *Ibid.*, II, p. 369 ; III. p. 190.

[3] *Ibid.*, II, p. 49.

recognize ourselves as such.   That is one of the great discords of
existence, and it is not resolvable.   If error is so necessary to
life, truth must be hostile to it.[1]   But how can a man consciously
remain in falsehood?   And if he must, is not death preferable?
There is no moral obligation attached to life.   That has been destroyed by the general point of view, just as much as has religion.[2]   The only motives left are pleasure and pain, utility and
injury, and they have nothing to do with a sense of truth.   They
are too closely bound together with errors.   "The whole of
human life is sunk deep in falsehood."   One cannot get away
from it, even for a moment; and once the circumstances are realized, one cannot avoid suspicion of everything, even that which
heretofore has been most sacred.   The result of such questioning
depends upon the temperament of the man concerned.   He may
despair, and adopt a philosophy of self-destruction; or he may
look upon life as if it were a play, cease to praise or blame, even
in thought, and live among men as if he were in the midst of
nature.   Only a good temperament makes the latter standpoint
possible, and any other finds all insight into truth and falsehood
unendurable.

The erroneous habits of thought extend to all the varieties of
mental activity, religious, ethical, æsthetic, and logical.   In the
discovery of the truth, the last-named is the most important; and
the account of its development is the history of philosophy.   The
fundamental difference between philosophy and science, which,
as we shall see later, is devoted to the investigation of truth *per
se*, is that philosophy always asks: What is the knowledge of
the world by which man lives most happily?[3]   This separation
between philosophy and science first took place in the Socratic
school, and ever since that time, philosophy has turned its attention exclusively to subjects directly or indirectly related to the
question of happiness.   All philosophers have the same fault,
in that they take the man of the present, and treat him as if he
were an *æterna veritas*.   In reality, everything that can be said

---

[1] *Op. cit.*, II, pp. 51, 370.
[2] *Ibid.*, II, p. 52.
[3] *Ibid.*, II, p. 22.

of man, refers merely to a limited period of his development. All the essential human characteristics were developed in the primitive ages, long before the four thousand years of which we know something. Perhaps in this comparatively recent period man has not changed much. The whole of teleology is built upon the assumption that the man of to-day is something eternally the same, toward whom all things in the world have a natural tendency. But there are no eternal facts, just as there are no absolute truths; and when one regards man as a changing being, the inclination to a teleological view ceases. For a recognition of this transitory nature a historical philosophy is needed.

One of the most fundamental of the philosophical assumptions is that of opposites; and it has led to the question as to how something can arise out of its opposite, *e. g.*, the reasonable out of the unreasonable, altruism from egoism.[1] The answer of metaphysical philosophy is the denial of the origin of one thing from another, and the assumption of a miraculous source for the things of higher value. Here is a place where historical philosophy has already done good service, in that it has discovered that, in certain cases, there are no opposites, except in the exaggerations of popular and metaphysical conceptions. This will doubtless prove to be the case everywhere, and the whole doctrine of opposites will be found to rest upon an error of reason.

Equally fundamental and equally false are related beliefs in the freedom of the will, in unconditioned substance, and in like (*gleich*) things.[2] The belief in substance has been called universal and original; but, like everything else, it has arisen only gradually. The lower organism sees everything as the same. Later, when the excitations of pleasure and pain become more noticeable, the different substances slowly become differentiated, each one with a single relation to the organism in question. At first nothing interests the latter, except pleasurable and painful relations to itself. Between these moments of sensation, everything seems to be changeless, alike. Perhaps the original belief of everything organic is that all the rest of the world is one and

---

[1] *Op. cit.*, II, pp. 17-19; III, p. 237.

[2] *Ibid.*, II, pp. 34-36; *Die fröhliche Wissenschaft*, V, p. 149.

unmoved. These beliefs, namely, in substance and in like or identical things, are transmitted to man from the early period in which they originated. Even when he has come to take a broader view of the world, he clings to the old beliefs, as to something true in themselves.

For the primitive stage of logic just described, the thought of causality in the usual sense is not present. All feelings and actions are still regarded as due to a free will. The individual looks upon every change in himself as something isolated and without connection with anything else. This is another fundamental error of everything organic. " In so far as all metaphysics has concerned itself with substance and freedom of the will, it may be called the science that treats of the fundamental errors of man as if they were fundamental truths."

The discovery of the laws of number rests upon the error that there are similar or identical things, or at least, that there are things ; but, in reality, there is nothing identical, and there are no things.[1] The assumption of multiplicity presupposes that there is something which appears multifariously ; and error is already present in the presupposition. It has invented unities which do not exist. Sensations of space and time are false, because they may be traced back to logical contradictions. In all scientific statements we reckon with false quantities ; but because these are constant, the results of science have a complete certainty in their interrelationship, up to the point where they come into contradiction with the erroneous assumptions. This is the case with atomism, where one is forced to assume a thing or a material substrate, while the whole scientific process has been engaged upon the question of resolving everything material into movement.

The error of regarding man as an unchanging entity has already been mentioned. The same tendency manifests itself in the assumption that the world is something fixed, with no process of development behind it. Philosophers look at life and experience, the world of phenomena as they call it, as if it were

[1] *Menschliches allzu Menschliches*, II, pp. 36, 37 ; *Die fröhliche Wissenschaft*, V, p. 149.

a painting once for all there, and as if their task were to understand it so thoroughly as to make possible an inference to the nature of the painter. Such a logical step from the effect to the cause, from the phenomenon to the unconditioned, which is always looked upon as its sufficient ground, disregards the strict meaning of the words. The unconditioned must also be the unconditioning, and so could have no connection with the phenomenon. There is no reason save the historical one, why we should try to explain the world from the thing-in-itself.[1] The world is our own invention. The reason why it is so many-colored, so terrible and full of deep meaning, is that for thousands of years we have looked at it from the standpoint of our moral, æsthetic, and religious demands. The human mind, on the basis of its own needs and emotions, has made the appearance appear, and has read its own erroneous conceptions into the things. Recently it has partially realized its mistake, and now men refuse to draw any more inferences from phenomena to the thing-in-itself; or else they demand the complete surrender of the human intellect and will, in order that by becoming themselves like the essence they may come nearer to it. Others accuse not the intellect but the nature of things, and preach deliverance from being. All these answers to the problem, however, like the problem itself, are to be explained historically.

The influence of the false inference from idea to objective existence is seen in other departments of thought than that of logic proper. Mathematics would never have arisen, if, at the beginning, man had not hypostasized his own ideas. He was interested in the perfect circles and absolute measures, because he thought that they really existed somewhere, quite independent of him. In the same way, the significance of language for the development of culture lies in the assumption that the concepts and name correspond to certain eternal truths; for a belief that truth has already been found is a great source of power. Fortunately, the mistake was discovered too late to retard the development of reason, which rests upon it.

These metaphysical errors, which have been so valuable in the

[1] *Op. cit.*, II, pp. 25, 26.

past, are still prized, because they put a meaning into unpleasant
things, and make self-dissatisfaction seem a part of the world-suf-
fering, the world-riddle.[1]   One feels oneself less responsible, and
finds external things more interesting.   When one is more ma-
ture, one comes to distrust the metaphysical method, and to see
that the same results would have been obtained just as well and
more scientifically by means of physics and history.   One must
discard metaphysics for science.   In some respects, it is true,
metaphysics may bring the greater happiness ; but it is a mark
of higher culture to prefer small truths reached by a strict
method to the errors of metaphysics and art, no matter how productive of pleasure the latter may be.[2]   That which has been
hardly won is certain and full of results for the future.   To cling
to it is manly and courageous.   Gradually not only the individual but all mankind will be lifted to this manliness.   The
first step is scepticism,[3] which will sometime be the prevailing
attitude.   " Belief in the truth begins with doubting all truths
hitherto believed."[4]   First, one must leave behind superstitions
and religious concepts, and after them, metaphysics.   The next
step is to understand the historical development.   One must know
the psychological justification of the ideas in question, and the
part that they have played in the past.   This is much more difficult than the other two steps, and fewer people are able to take
it.   As soon as the origin of religion, art, and morals, is so described that their problems can be explained without metaphysical assumptions, then the chief interest of theoretical questions is
gone.   There is no place left for them to fill.   Their function
has been usurped by the different branches of science.   The separation of the world picture from its essence is referred to physi-
ology and the genetic history of organizations and concepts.[5]
Such a study leads to the conviction that what is called the
world is the result of a mass of errors which have gradually
arisen during the past, and which have been inherited by each
successive generation.   They are of the utmost value, because

[1] *Op. cit.*, II, pp. 33, 34.   [4] *Ibid.*, III, p. 22.
[2] *Ibid.*, II, pp. 19–21.   [5] *Ibid.*, II, pp. 24, 25, 33.
[3] *Ibid.*, II, pp. 38, 39.

the whole worth of humanity rests upon them : without them the world and human life would be a shadow with neither permanence nor meaning. A recognition of the significance of these errors, however, forms no argument against endeavoring to understand their origin. To a certain extent a knowledge of them enables one to escape the delusions that they offer, but the very necessities of life make this possible only to a small degree.

In fact, there is a disadvantage attendant upon the cessation of metaphysical views. The individual who puts them aside is prone to pay too much attention to his own life and impulses, and no longer to take any interest in permanent institutions, which will first become valuable in the future.[1] He wishes to gain all the advantages for himself, and has not much regard for posterity. The influence of metaphysics tends to destroy this tendency ; for it presupposes that the absolute truth is known, and is in some way closely connected with the individual. All that he does for the cause of truth is necessarily to his own advantage. For instance, if he builds a church, he is furthering the eternal safety of his soul. Science, on the other hand, brings suspicion with it. The only feasible method of work takes the form of an attempt to unite the advantages of both science and metaphysics.[2] The value of illusion and error is that they provide fuel for the fire, so to speak. Without the pleasures that they bring, one has no interest in the pursuit of knowledge. It is possible to divide one's mind between the two, to allow metaphysics and the feelings accompanying it to influence the affective side of mental life, to provide the motive, and on the other hand, to keep the intellectual pursuits more or less free from metaphysical methods.[3] Some such division is necessary, for without it no pleasure would be connected with the investigation of truth, and it would therefore cease.

It must not be thought, that, in renouncing the more pretentious questions of metaphysics and the promises of religion, one is left entirely without recompense for their loss.[4] In comparison with such brilliant possibilities, the aim of modern science,

---

[1] *Op. cit.*, II, pp. 39, 40.   [2] *Ibid.*, II, pp. 235, 236.
[3] *Ibid.*, III, p. 20.   [4] *Ibid.*, II, p. 133.

namely, as little pain as possible for the individual coupled with
long life, seems tame and of little worth ; but, for the present, at
least, scientific work is invested with a charm, which its rivals
cannot offer.[1]   Its principles are yet to be established ; and the
laws and methods that characterize its different branches, are,
almost without exception, still being sought.   Instead of going
over territory already travelled, the scientist has the pleasure of
exploring new provinces heretofore unknown.   Even apart from
the joy of discovery, however, which will inevitably be lessened
as knowledge progresses, all pursuit of science is pleasurable.
Scientific men often defend themselves against objections from the
side of religion by pointing out the life of renunciation and self-
sacrifice which they are obliged to lead.   Among themselves
they are more honorable.   If science were distasteful to them, or,
perhaps, even if there were no practical advantages attendant upon
it, they would not devote themselves to it.   In other words, if
they were not to some extent unscientific men, science would
hold nothing for them. [2]

A detailed discussion of Nietzsche's criticisms of metaphysics,
and of the position that he gives to science, is rendered impossible by the vague nature of his statements.   The treatment is
so brief and fragmentary, the interrelationship between the different subjects is so wholly ignored, that one is never certain of his
exact meaning.   He mentions a theory, states perhaps one objection, and dismisses the matter as forever settled, often without
giving his reasons or even making clear exactly what it is to
which he objects.   It is necessary, therefore, to confine oneself
to a criticism of his method as a whole.   There are certain characteristics displayed all through the discussions of metaphysical
questions ; and since these are typical of his general attitude, it
seems no injustice to Nietzsche to select them for remark rather
than the details.

The first criticism to be made upon the standpoint as a whole,
is that Nietzsche makes a double assumption.   He constantly
presupposes the existence of absolute truth, and just as con-

[1] *Op. cit.*, II, pp. 239, 240.
[2] *Ibid.*, III, pp. 55, 56.

stantly denies it. He regards truth as the one thing worth while, the one standard by which everything must be judged; but he asserts also that the whole history of humanity, its valuations included, is built upon error. He assumes that it is possible to get away from the human mind, to stand off at one side as it were, observe its methods of thought and feeling, and judge them as true or false, good or bad. Now this assumption is one that in some form is undoubtedly made in all epistemology. Logic and, to a certain extent, metaphysics are impossible without it. The mind cannot judge its own activities without abstracting from itself, and seeming to place itself, as its object, outside of itself. To condemn such a procedure is to condemn all possible philosophy. It is not the method that is at fault, but the nature of the standard employed. So long as this is found within the mind no objection can be made to the assumption that would not apply as well to all mental valuations; but when one supposes the standard to be altogether apart from the human mind, one gets into trouble, and it is here that Nietzsche's assumption must be rejected as unjustifiable. Of course, he did not explicitly affirm the existence of a standard of truth outside the mind; but he makes its existence within the mind an impossibility. He has the standard ready made; but he nowhere explains where he gets it, and how he could separate himself from human methods of thought sufficiently to be able to use it. Everything else, all the opinions and methods of religion, morality, and philosophy, are the results of a long course of development which has led to error, not to truth. If the idea of truth itself has the same origin, it should, to say the least, be received with suspicion. If it has not, then how, with Nietzsche's presuppositions, does it come to exist at all? He constantly implies a standard in his references to error. Moreover, he expressly states that there is some standard, and makes his whole standpoint depend upon it. Certainly he would be the last to deny that human ideas as to the nature of truth, are often incorrect; but all these he relegates to the domain of metaphysics. His own truth seems to be something entirely different, but just what it is, he nowhere tells us. If all methods and forms of logic are to be regarded as erroneous, and valuable only in that they help to preserve the race, then not only all standards of truth but even the forms of thought, including those employed by Nietzsche in his condemnation of metaphysics, must be rejected. One cannot regard the human mind as the result of a gradual evolution, and yet reserve certain ideas and activities for a more absolute evaluation, or suppose the part of the mind that judges the evolution is not itself the result of development. There are no standards other than those furnished by the mind itself, and if intellectual evolution is logically false, so are the standards upon which the judgment is based.

This leads to the second criticism of this portion of Nietzsche's work. He constantly implies, both here and elsewhere, that whatever can be described historically is to that extent explained and evaluated. No real and permanent worth can be ascribed to anything that has been proven to have its historical origin in utility of some sort, or, one might almost say, to anything that has had an origin at all. The genetic problem is constantly confused with those of essence and value. If a metaphysical theory has been developed gradually, and owes its origin and preservation to some strictly utilitarian service which it has rendered to the human race, it is thereby, so far as ultimate worth is concerned, swept forever out of existence. No further question as to its rational justification can possibly arise. Now the problems of origin may undoubtedly throw light upon that of essence, and still more upon that of value ; but it is not the same as either, and any attempt to merge the three must lead to confusion.

What were the reasons, then, that led Nietzsche to adopt these views of epistemology ? He was a careful thinker, and not likely to err through mere heedlessness. His opinions must have had some positive value in themselves, something that, in spite of fundamental defects, make them worthy of consideration. Of course they were not final, and he later found cause to modify them ; but, nevertheless, they were his during the intellectual period, just as much as if he had never changed them an iota. No man regards his own theories as transitional, no matter how often he may see fit to discard them and adopt new ones. Those that Nietzsche finally left to the world, as distinctively his, are so only by chance ; if time or opportunity had offered, he would probably have changed them again. Transitional period and final form differ only in degree, and to a certain extent are to be judged by the same standards. The intellectual stage of Nietzsche's philosophy must stand for something more than its relation to the succeeding and final period.

When one comes to think of it, is there not something to be said for this attitude of extreme scepticism, in spite of its glaring contradictions ? When a man has once begun to question accepted truth, why should he stop short of the end ? The relentless force of logic pushes him on and on, until he must doubt his doubts. It is not the position of the builder of a constructive system, but it surely is no unthinkable attitude. In certain ages it is not even unusual. The mind that is capable of rigid questioning up to a certain point, but can stop before it reaches the inevitable self-contradictions ahead of less happily-constructed thinkers, is surely blessed with a nice equilibrium between the destructive and constructive elements. Nietzsche did not belong to these well-balanced minds, but it is something not to be afraid of contradictions. Not every sceptic dares to follow his scepticism no matter where it leads him.

Sec. 2. Culture.

The culture built upon a scientific basis, which Nietzsche regarded as the *summum bonum*, finds its representative figure in the "free spirit" (*Freigeist*). Such a culture has certain indispensable prerequisites. The first of these is frequent war.[1] It is mere fantastic dreaming to suppose that mankind will ever cease to wage wars, or that, if such a universal peace should be brought to pass, it would be a benefit. Culture cannot dispense with the strong passions, the force and swiftness of hand and brain, the readiness to fight for oneself, the barbarity, if you like, which war brings with it. Permanent peace would mean physical and mental enervation, and would at last bring about the destruction of the race.

Another necessary condition for a high grade of culture is the

[1] *Menschliches allzu Menschliches*, II, pp. 229, 355, 356; III, p. 295.

existence of two social castes, that of the laborers and that of the men of leisure.[1]   Society must be organized in such a way that those who have capacity for leisure are enabled to attain it. The division must not be so iron bound that no transference of the individual is possible.   It should be elastic enough to allow a free interchange from either class to the other.   Such an arrangement, by which the most difficult labor and privations are given to the men who will suffer least thereby, that is, to the most stupid, and then are gradually lessened until they reach those for whom life is difficult under any circumstances—this Nietzsche calls his " Utopia." [2]

A third prerequisite for culture, on a rather different level from the other two, but no less important, is the occasional degeneration of certain of the members of society.[3]   A race maintains itself best, when the individuals composing it follow the customs of the majority, and cling to common convictions and beliefs. This community of opinion and habit strengthens the subordination of the individual to society, and brings about firmness of character.   The accompanying danger is that the inherited stability will become stupidity.   On this account, if a high grade of culture is to arise, society needs occasional weaker members, sometimes even madmen.   Most of these will undoubtedly perish through their lack of conformity to the general custom ; but here and there will appear some one who manages to preserve his existence, and who introduces a new element into the state of society in which he finds himself.   He is followed by others of the same stamp, who strengthen the tendency that he has introduced.   The weaker natures are indispensable to progress.

This is the historical significance of the free spirit.   He is the reverse of what is usually called a strong character.[4]   His actions do not have the quickness and the certainty of his mentally more limited neighbor, because, instead of choosing between three or four motives, he must select from a great number.   How can he

[1] *Op. cit.*, II, p. 327.
[2] *Ibid.*, II, pp. 340, 341.
[3] *Ibid.*, II, pp. 211, 213 ; *Morgenröte*, IV, pp. 21–23.
[4] *Menschliches allzu Menschliches*, II, pp. 216–218.

act quickly, when he sees perhaps fifty possibilities? Another of his characteristics is that he is constantly changing his opinions.[1] He has no convictions; whoever desires mental freedom must avoid any permanent form of ideas. He regards some things as certain, and others as probable, but he has nothing properly answering to beliefs. The exact nature of his opinions is not of so much importance in determining the degree of freedom he has attained, as is the method through which he reached them. A man is free who thinks otherwise than might have been expected from his original surroundings and station, or from the prevailing opinions of the time.[2] He is always the exception, and wherever he differs from his fellows he is probably in the right. The one essential thing is entire independence of prevailing ideas. It is only of secondary importance whether he reached his views through moral or immoral means, or whether they are in themselves right or wrong. Not what he thinks, but how he thinks, is the standard by which he must be judged; and the same rule holds good not only for his thinking but also for his actions.

Nevertheless, although on the whole he may think as he likes,[3] yet there are certain opinions that he cannot hold and remain free. For instance, his position with regard to Christianity must be critical. Probably the time will come when one will prefer the *Memorabilia* of Socrates to the Bible, and will gain more profit from its perusal.[4] To be really cultured, too, a man must be able to vibrate between the greatest strictness of method in matters of knowledge and a whole-souled devotion to poetry, religion, and metaphysics.[5] This is not to be regarded as wavering; it is more like dancing, which Nietzsche considers as the highest of the arts. Advancing freedom of thought, together with modern commercial and literary conditions, will doubtless weaken the present feeling of nationality.[6] The free spirit of the future will not belong to any particular nation, but will call himself instead a " good European."

[1] *Op. cit.*, II, p. 412.
[2] *Ibid.*, II, pp. 213, 214.
[3] *Ibid.*, III, p. 292.
[4] *Ibid.*, III, pp. 248, 249.
[5] *Ibid.*, II, p. 258.
[6] *Ibid.*, II, pp. 252, 253.

Closely related to the problem of the free spirit, is that of the production of genius. History testifies that genius arises only after centuries of trouble, toil and conflict, and then only under certain conditions.[1] It is possible that the more special elements conditioning its rise, belong to a limited period of time. Genius, in the accepted sense of the word, is strictly dependent upon states of mind that are doomed, sooner or later, to perish. Religious feeling, for instance, has had its time ; and much that was good in the past can never come again, because its proper soil is no longer there. In the future, there will be no religious limit to the horizon of life and culture. The saint, who requires a certain limitation of intellect, is gone forever. Force and strength, the pleasure in action, the delight in deception, in everything symbolic, in intoxication and ecstasy, all these are dying or already dead, and their good effects must perish with them. If the socialists should ever establish their state, which is to be based upon the good of the greatest number, opportunities for genius would be at once destroyed. There would be no occasion for the energy that conditions great intellect.[2] If life once loses its character of force, if it once becomes as pleasant and easy as kind-hearted people would like to make it, it will, at the same time, become valueless. The greatest happiness for the multitude and the production of genius are incompatible, and a society containing both is an impossibility.

Sec. 3. Æsthetics.

Many of the metaphysical propositions, which have been condemned from the logical point of view, are absolutely indispensable to the development of art.[3] The assumption, for instance, that character is unchangeable, and that the essence of the world expresses itself in human actions, is of the greatest value to the artist. His work thereby becomes a picture of the permanent. If he discards the theory, art ceases to have the same meaning for him, and becomes transitory, of value only for one age. In

[1] *Op. cit.*, II, pp. 219–221, 226.
[2] *Ibid.*, II, pp. 221–223.
[3] *Ibid.*, II, pp. 200, 201, 206, 207.

the same way, the theory that the visible world is only phenomenon, is of æsthetic importance. The artistic world seems then to approach the actual, and art comes to represent the prototype of nature rather than a mere copy of it. With the fall of these metaphysical doctrines, art must eventually take a lower position. At present its status depends upon the tenacity with which we still cling to the feelings connected with former opinions, even when the opinions themselves have been rejected.[1] Even the free spirit finds it difficult to say good-bye to these feelings, which express a need of the nature he has inherited. The Ninth Symphony of Beethoven brings back the dream of immortality even to the most enlightened mind. The proper function of art is to satisfy the longings felt during the transition from the religious to the scientific point of view.[2] Philosophy may take the place of art, and supply some of the acquired needs caused by religion, but art is much better for the purpose, because it preserves in a less degree the ideas to be discarded. The proper course of development is from religion to art, and from art to science.[3]

Sec. 4. Religion.

Between religion and science there is no kinship. In fact, they lie in such wholly different spheres that there is not even hostility between them. All religions are the product of anxiety and need, ·and are based upon erroneous reasoning. Any philosophical theory to be found in one of them is not to be regarded as an element of the religion proper. It did not make its appearance until religion was threatened by science, and is a theological work of art, the product of a time when religion had already begun to doubt itself. " No religion has ever, mediately or immediately, either as dogma or as symbol, contained a truth." They are all composed of errors from beginning to end. The common consent of mankind, which has often been advanced as an argument for religion, is in fact one of the reasons for rejecting it. Nothing but foolishness is believed by everybody. The

[1] *Op. cit.*, II, pp. 160–162.
[2] *Ibid.*, II, p. 45.
[3] *Ibid.*, II, p. 207.

cause for the influence of religion is to be sought in the past.   Religious life was strongest, at a time when little was known of nature or her laws [1] and when there was not the slightest conception of natural causality.   In those days nothing in the external world seemed to be certain.   Everywhere one saw only caprice and the rule of chance.   Illness and death were thought to be the results of magic influence.   The one exception to the general instability was man.   Since his actions were ruled by a few well-known motives, they could usually be foreseen.   This feeling of contrast between man and the world is the fundamental conviction that lies at the basis of all religious creeds.   To the modern man, on the contrary, nature is the rule, and he is the caprice.   Human life has become individualized, and is no longer all made on the same pattern, as it was in primitive times.   Among savage races, everything is determined by law and custom ; even the simplest acts of everyday life are so firmly fixed that their performance becomes almost automatic.   Nature, on the other hand, is the realm of freedom.   It is a superhuman stage of existence, that is, God.   The savage feels that his own happiness as well as that of his neighbors depends upon this uncertain quantity ; and the problem that he attempts to solve is to make it as law abiding as he is himself.   The result is the rise of religious worship, by means of which he hopes to dictate laws to the higher powers. This is to be brought about, in the first place, by the kind of compulsion that comes through personal inclination.   If the savage by prayers and gifts can win the favor of his God, he is safe.   He feels that they have made a contract.   Of more importance, however, is the compulsion that is the result of incantations.   Just as a man can injure his enemies by the help of magic, so he can determine the action of the spirits of nature.   After a time, with the growth of religion, confusion arises among the great number of rules and ceremonies, and it is found necessary to systematize them.   The magician becomes the priest.   Before religion has reached this stage, however, other elements besides incantation and sacrifice have been influential.   One must presuppose some tie between the different members of society, the

[1] *Op. cit.*, II, pp. 120–125.

existence of many of the social virtues, and also the feeling of shame before a mystery, the belief that there is something divine which can be touched only under certain conditions and by certain people.[1]

In the formation of the separate religions, deception has played a large part ; but before they can grow, its rôle must have been subordinated to others.[2] The deceiver must become the deceived, if his influence is to be either broad or permanent. All great deceptions end in deceiving the deceiver. The founder of a religion is distinguished from other falsifiers only in one point, namely, that having once succeeded in deceiving himself, he never emerges from this condition. He ascribes his clearer moments to the influence of the evil one. His own enthusiasm is contagious, and communicates itself to others. The religion gains adherents, most of whom it owes to the happiness that it brings with it.[3] This beneficial result, although the chief cause of its growth, is no argument for its truth, as its advocates have usually imagined. A belief can not be of much value if it is accepted only because it brings pleasure. However, the feelings thus arising are wonderfully permanent.[4] When all religious belief is gone, the religious mood often remains. Many a free spirit who objects strongly to religious doctrines is well acquainted with the magic of religious feelings. It takes a strong intellectual conscience to be able to reject so much that one longs to keep, and yet cannot honorably retain.[5]

Nietzsche's treatment of Christianity, to which he devotes much space and not a little harsh language, perhaps does not logically belong to a discussion that professes to include only his philosophy. The influence that he has exercised, however, especially upon the popular mind, has been largely due to these anti-Christian opinions ; and, for that reason, it may not be out of place to devote some brief consideration to them. Nietzsche's criticism may be divided into two main heads : first, Christianity is false ; sec-

[1] *Op. cit.*, II, pp. 101, 102.
[2] *Ibid.*, II, pp. 74, 76, 77, 130, 131 ; *Morgenröte*, IV, pp. 61, 62.
[3] *Menschliches allzu Menschliches*, II, p. 130.
[4] *Ibid.*, II, pp. 133–135.
[5] *Ibid.*, II, pp. 116, 117.

ond, assuming that it is true, Christians do not live in accordance with the rules laid down for them. In the discussion of the first point, he insists that Christianity is only a temporary form of religion, and will disappear sooner or later.[1] It is utterly and frankly illogical ; it desires belief and belief only, and rejects every demand for reasons. " Believe," it says, " and you will be happy." [2] That is, it regards the personal utility of an opinion as proof of its truth. Moreover, it is inconsistent with itself. For instance, prayer is reasonable only under two assumptions : (1) that it is possible to change the determination of the divinity, and (2) that the petitioner is the best judge of what he needs.[3] Both suppositions, which are accepted in all other religions, are denied by Christianity ; but, nevertheless, prayer is retained. This logical inconsistency, unjustifiable as it is from the intellectual point of view, displays, nevertheless, great cleverness. In the Christian formula, *ora et labora*, prayer takes the place of enjoyment. Without it, what would the saints, those unhappy men who could not work, have done ? But to talk with God and demand pleasant things from him, to make a little sport, as if one could be so foolish as to have wishes in spite of such a father, that, according to Nietzsche, was a most happy discovery for the saint. Another clever artifice is the doctrine of complete sinfulness, which lessens the feeling of personal responsibility. [4] No matter what crimes a man may commit, he sins, not as an individual, but as a member of humanity in general, and so differs little from his fellows. Again, the dogma that Christian virtue is attainable, materially increases human happiness. The belief that one loves one's enemies, even though it rests upon no psychological foundation, is productive of an extremely comfortable state of mind. [5] If an evil exists, Christianity does not try to destroy it, but merely to change the opinion regarding it, and to make it seem to be a good.[6] Christianity is therefore a narcotic, not a remedy.

[1] *Op. cit.*, III, p. 53.
[2] *Ibid.*, II, pp. 215, 216.
[3] *Ibid.*, III, pp. 242, 243.
[4] *Ibid.*, II, p. 128.
[5] *Ibid.*, III, pp. 52, 53.
[6] *Ibid.*, II, pp. 115, 116.

Its strongest point is the emphasis that it places upon love.[1]   It is a lyrical religion, and so makes an appeal to the heart.

The imperfections of Christianity are most apparent when it is compared with the Hellenic religion.[2]   The Greeks did not regard their gods as of a different nature from themselves, but as the most perfect examples of their own race.   Christianity, on the other hand, is a religion of slaves.   The relation between a Christian and his God is that between vassal and master, something barbaric and ignoble.   There may have been a time when Christianity was beneficial.[3]   At the close of antiquity, when philosophy had lost its influence, and corruption was at its height, there may have been some value in the sight of men who were more soul than body, and who, in waiting for a better life, had become so proudly scornful of this one ; but for fresh young barbarian peoples Christianity was poison.   The doctrines of sinfulness and damnation were of the utmost injury to them.   At present, the only way in which Christianity should be regarded, is as a bit of ancient history, which has no further significance. " When on a Sunday morning we hear the old bells ring, we ask ourselves : Is it possible ! that is for a Jew who was crucified two thousand years ago, and who said he was the son of God. The proof of such a statement is lacking."[4]

The second division of Nietzsche's polemic against Christianity he disposes of more briefly.   If Christianity were right in its doctrines of a revengeful God, universal depravity, election by grace, and the danger of eternal damnation, it would be a sign of weak intellect and lack of character to live as an ordinary Christian does.   If he really believes his creed, how can he avoid becoming a priest or a hermit?   How can he devote himself to anything else than to the working out with fear and trembling of his own salvation ?   Either he must be a hypocrite, who does not really believe what he professes ; or else he is a fool, so great a fool that he does not deserve to be punished with such severity

---

[1] *Ibid.*, III, pp. 51, 52.
[2] *Ibid.*, II, pp. 127, 128.
[3] *Ibid.*, III, pp. 122–124.
[4] *Ibid.*, pp. 126, 127.

as Christianity threatens. The joyful side of the Christian religion, too, finds just as little confirmation in the lives of its professors.[1] If the glad message of the Bible were written in their faces, they would not need to believe so obstinately in its divine authority. Their words and actions would be continually producing a new Bible. All apologies for Christianity have their root in the unchristianity of Christians.

All this charge of inconsistency is doubtless justified by the facts. It has been made many times before. Nietzsche is one of a large body of learned men, numerous in all countries, but perhaps nowhere more so than in Germany, who find nothing to praise and everything to blame in the existing religion. That much is to be said for their position is scarcely to be denied; but one may question whether it is strengthened by an intolerance even more unyielding than that which they blame in their opponents.

Nietzsche's criticisms upon religion in general are interesting, more because they are characteristic of his attitude, than from any great originality that they display. In especial, the place that is accorded to voluntary deception reminds one forcibly of the theories of the eighteenth century. Nevertheless, it is evident that Nietzsche's views upon this subject are the direct result of his intellectualistic theory of valuation. The most scathing criticism he can bring against religion in general and Christianity in particular is that neither is true. Later, as will be seen, he placed more emphasis upon their enervating results, but during the period under discussion, anything that was branded as unscientific had received the climax of condemnation; and, though the evil results following it might be noted, they never received more than a minor share of the blame.

Sec. 5. Ethics.

The relation between Nietzsche's general attitude and his theories upon ethics is not so close as it is in the case of religion. He attempts to show that the prevailing moral distinctions are false, and that they have passed through a course

[1] *Ibid.,* III, p. 56.

of development analogous to that of the logical concepts; but he is continually appealing to standards that belong more properly to the succeeding period, in that they are more fully in agreement with the other theories to be found there. The starting point for the discussion of morality is furnished by his opposition to Schopenhauer's doctrine of the basal nature of sympathy. According to Nietzsche, sympathy, instead of being the basis of moral action, is a sign of weakness.[1] In order that it may be effective, there must be some one to receive it, that is, some one who is not only suffering, but who is unable to help himself.[2] It is a poor kind of morality that depends upon pain and weakness in others for its very existence. Besides, why should it be a virtue to offer to others what one regards as an insult, when proffered to oneself? No proud man desires sympathy. Why should he think so poorly of others as to inflict it upon them? Sympathy is a sign of contempt, and is essentially indelicate. The sympathetic man stoops to the object of his thoughtfulness, and meddles with matters that do not concern him. Such a course of action is advocated principally by the incompetent, who must receive assistance from others. Sympathy, instead of being beneficial, is positively harmful, because it increases suffering.[3]

The defense of sympathy that is based upon its supposedly unselfish nature is not justified by the facts.[4] Sympathy is always exhibited in the satisfaction of an impulse the denial of which would give pain. The sympathetic man is no more unselfish than is his unsympathetic neighbor. Both obey the dictates of their own natures. Even the element of self-sacrifice does not make sympathy moral.[5] In every action some part of the self is sacrificed to another. It is impossible to satisfy all the desires at once, some must yield. Yet no one would maintain that such subordination in itself renders an action moral.

[1] *Ibid.*, II, p. 70.

[2] *Ibid.*, III, pp. 228, 230, 236.

[3] *Morgenröte*, IV, p. 139.

[4] *Menschliches allzu Menschliches*, pp. 78, 79, 105, 106; *Morgenröte*, IV, pp. 137, 138.

[5] *Menschliches allzu Menschliches*, III, p. 32.

Curiously enough, our idea of sympathy has always been limited to a participation in the pain of others, rather than in their pleasure. True, the latter is more rarely found, but it is valuable in a corresponding degree.[1] One might almost call it the distinguishing mark of genuine friendship.[2] Even the little courtesies of everyday life are preferable to sympathy in the ordinary sense of the word.[3] They are egoistic, to be sure, but the emphasis that has been laid upon the altruistic nature of sympathy proceeds from the mistaken assumption that egoism is immoral. On the contrary, there is nothing which is bad in itself. Some actions are stupid, but none of them are bad. No one ever desires evil for its own sake. Whatever is done for the sake of self-preservation is usually called bad, because it often interferes with the maintenance of other people;[4] but if one once admits that self-defense is moral, then all egoistic action must be placed in the same category. There is no reason for making a distinction at any particular point. In fact, the different grades of morality are only lower or higher forms of egoism.[5] It is an impossibility to imagine an action that is not egoistic. Even in the most sincere attempt to live a purely altruistic life, it is necessary to do countless things for oneself, before one can be of any use to others. For the ego to act apart from the ego is a contradiction in terms. The life of the ascetic, for instance, is in reality egoistic.[6] He submits himself to a set of rules, to which he rigidly adheres; but he does it for the purpose of making life as easy as possible. It is much more difficult to observe moderation in the satisfaction of the desires and passions, than to deny them altogether; just as it is harder to decide for oneself than to leave the decision to others. More than that, the ascetic is usually a man who is tired of life—one who has tried all the ordinary pleasures and means of excitement and exhausted them. Stringency toward himself is the only way in which he

[1] *Op. cit.*, II, p. 276, III, p. 41; *Die fröhliche Wissenschaft*, V, p. 263.
[2] *Menschliches allzu Menschliches*, II, p. 366.
[3] *Ibid.*, II, pp. 70, 71.
[4] *Ibid.*, II, pp. 100, 101.
[5] *Ibid.*, II, pp. 66, 67, 137.
[6] *Ibid.*, II, pp. 141–152.

can make life interesting. His method differs from that of the voluptuary, but neither has the advantage over the other in the amount of egoism displayed. Another motive for asceticism is the desire for power. Some men have so great a need for expressing their own strength that, in default of other people to rule, they select certain portions of their own nature and tyrannize over them. The value and influence of such men depends less upon what they are than what they signify. The saint of history owed his extraordinary power to the mistaken idea concerning him held by the unsaintly portion of the community. He was not a particularly good man, still less particularly wise, but he seemed to them to stand for a goodness and wisdom that transcended all human measurement. He gave support to their belief in the divine and miraculous. It was only their prejudice that prevented them from seeing the strong egoistic element in sainthood.

In fact, the truly moral man is the egoist *par excellence.* His distinguishing characteristic is force. He wishes to stand and fall alone, with no interference from sympathetic bystanders. He thinks and acts for himself. Everything, in order to have worth for him, must be strong. He would rather have a great pain than a small pleasure. He is not troubled with any feelings of responsibility or sinfulness. He knows that there is no such thing as sin,[1] and that no one is responsible.[2] He does not take the happiness of the greatest number as the basis of his judgments of worth, because he realizes that no one can choose happiness for another person ; that people with different ideals and different standpoints do not enjoy the same things and never will. The development of his own personality is the one important thing to him, and such a development presupposes a constant exercise of power. This brings with it more or less pleasure in the injury of other people.[3] Nearly all the everyday actions have something of this element in them. For instance, the pleasure of teasing ceases with the annoyance of the person subjected to it.

[1] *Op. cit.,* II, pp. 77, 78, 131.
[2] *Ibid.,* II, pp. 96, 109–112.
[3] *Ibid.,* II, pp. 72, 73, 105, 106; III, pp. 213, 214.

One of the great errors in ethics is the assumption of the free-dom of the will.   In the first place, such a freedom presupposes isolated acts, which do not exist.[1]   Experience is something continuous.   It is impossible to isolate any single term and re-gard it as existing in and for itself.   What is really meant by freedom is the absence of all feeling of dependence, and such a state of mind is surely no proof that the dependence does not exist.   Every one thinks he is free at the point where he has most power ; and so some men are convinced of the existence of freedom by one class of acts, others by another class.[2]   There are two reasons why libertarianism has been defended so fiercely. The first is that men have feared determinism ;[3] they have con-fused it with fatalism, and supposed that it would bring with it a weakening of the power of initiative.   The second reason is the conviction that, since sin exists, there must be a sinner whose free will renders him responsible for his evil deeds.[4]   The feeling of sinfulness, however, is an error.   There is no sin.   The doc-trine was introduced by the Christian religion, and the two stand or fall together.[5]   Suppose there was no such thing, and that every one's conscience was perfectly clear !   The world would still be bad enough, but it would certainly be a much pleasanter place than it is now.

The whole theory of punishment and reward is utterly ir-reconcileable with libertarianism.[6]   If the criminal acts without a motive, that is, purely from chance, and if his crime is not the result of his character, he does not deserve to be punished.   In fact, punishment is justified only by its utility to society ; and to make it an argument for libertarianism, as so many writers upon ethics have done, shows a complete misunderstanding of the question.

The present standards of morality, then, and the theories with regard to them, are all false, but it must not be supposed that

---

[1] *Op. cit.*, III, pp. 195–198.
[2] *Ibid.*, II, pp. 108, 109.
[3] *Ibid.*, III, p. 235.
[4] *Ibid.*, III, pp. 30–32, 35.
[5] *Ibid.*, II, pp. 145–149.
[6] *Ibid.*, III, pp. 209–211. Hume and J. S. Mill present much the same argument.

their erroneous nature renders them any less beneficial to the development of human society. Like their counterparts in logic and religion, they have been of the utmost value in the elevation of the human race. In fact, the present views of what is moral or immoral find their basis in utility.[1] In the beginning this was always the utility of society. Whatever was good for the social organism, whatever helped it to exist and be strong, was regarded as morally good; whatever injured it was bad. Whenever, as often happened, the utility of the individual conflicted with that of the state, the former was looked upon as immoral. The long inherited distrust of the utility of the individual has extended itself to the whole field of the useful, so that at present there is a strong dislike to making even the most general utility the basis of moral judgment.

Upon analysis, the early notion of what constitutes utility and so moral worth, is found to be made up of two judgments:[2] (1) the community is worth more than the individual; (2) the permanent advantage is to be preferred to the transitory. At different times, under different conditions of society, different acts and dispositions are felt to be beneficial; but the good of society is always the standard by which they are judged. When a custom has once been established, its preservation is aided by the pleasure that it affords. The habitual is always easier to do than what is new and strange, and the very fact that it has preserved itself is an argument for its usefulness.[3] The primitive standard according to which acts are classified as good or bad, useful or injurious, is not the distinction between egoism and altruism, but rather that between the customary and the strange. Anything new is likely to be dangerous. Some customs, indeed, seem to have no other object than the maintenance of custom. Naturally, different classes of society find different actions useful.[4] The ruling caste, whose members are proud and warlike, does not desig-

---

[1] *Op. cit.*, III, pp. 50, 224, 225; *Morgenröte*, IV, pp. 96, 97.
[2] *Menschliches allzu Menschliches*, III, p. 49.
[3] *Ibid.*, II, pp. 97–99; *Morgenröte*, IV, pp. 15–19, 28.
[4] *Morgenröte*, IV, p. 24.

nate its enemies as bad.[1]   An enemy is a necessity, and the braver the enemy, the better he serves the purpose.   The term bad is applied to the coward.   A lower class, on the other hand, does not share in this feeling.   Every individual finds all the others dangerous to him ; everything not himself seems to him to be bad. Such a state of internal warfare is so destructive of life that a society in which it rules cannot long survive ; and the present standard of morality is that derived from the ruling class.

---

[1] *Menschliches allzu Menschliches,* II, pp. 68, 69 ; *Die fröhliche Wissenschaft,* V p. 156.

CHAPTER IV.

THE ETHICAL PERIOD.

The third period of Nietzsche's philosophy is the one which presents the greatest elements of originality, and for that reason it is of far more importance than the other two. On its negative side, that is, in the destructive criticism of existing standards, it does not differ much from the preceding period, except that it is more radical and uncompromising. The positive theories, on the other hand, almost without exception, now appear for the first time. In the one, the critical acumen is concentrated; in the other, all the artist's nice feeling for unity and harmony. Both tendencies are stronger than before, but instead of each playing havoc with the other, they are kept apart. The result is less inherent contradiction, and an artistic regard for] proportion that reaches its climax in *Also sprach Zarathustra*. In the following discussion only those subjects will be considered that offer some change from the views already described.

Perhaps at the beginning some justification of the heading of this chapter may not be amiss. Nietzsche is so often regarded as the man who tried to overthrow all moral valuations, that, at first thought, it seems absurd to call his theories ethical. What he attempted, however, was not the destruction of all moral standards, but merely of those dominant in modern civilization. He does not deny the right of all morality to existence. Perhaps it is not too much to say that five-sixths of all his published writings are devoted to the question of conduct. The doctrine which he made the center of his system, and which he proclaimed with almost religious fervor, namely, that of the Over-man, is altogether an ethical idea. It furnishes an aim and a standard for conduct.

Sec. 1. Truth.

The same question with which Nietzsche was so much concerned during the second period still claims his attention. On the whole, his treatment of it has become more satisfactory. He no longer makes the true the *summum bonum,* but asks boldly why man should prefer it to falsehood.[1]　There are no absolute and universal truths.　No one can go beyond what is true for himself.　Intellectual individualism makes any objective standard an impossibility.　Indeed the desire for such a standard is a mistake.　A man should be too proud to be willing to accept his neighbor's truth, or even to share his own with someone else. It is bad taste to wish to agree with many people.　There can be no common good, for what is common has little value.

There is no such thing as pure intellect.[2]　Most conscious thinking is secretly guided by the instincts that further life.[3]　Behind all logic stands the physiological demand for a particular kind of life.　A thought comes when it will, and not when I will.[4]　It is false to say that the subject *I* conditions the predicate *think.*　One can just as well say, *It thinks.*　Some day even the *it* may be counted among the superfluities.　Perhaps the whole thing, reality and appearance, may be only a fiction, an instance of the hypostasization of ideas that we have ourselves imagined.　If the apparent world were destroyed, there would be no truth left.　The opposition between the two is a gratuitous assumption.

Suppose that nothing is given as real except the desires and passions, that we know no other reality than that of our impulses.　Would not this be sufficient to understand the mechanical or material world, and to give it as much reality as our own affections possess?　The world would be a simpler, stronger prototype of life, in which all the organic functions are bound together.　Such an attempt at simplification is demanded by scientific method, which decrees that one shall not assume more kinds of causes than are absolutely necessary.　If the will is once recognized as causal in its nature, then the attempt must be made, hypothetically at least, to establish the will as the only causality.　Will can work only upon will, and all mechanical events must be regarded as exhibiting its power and effects.　If,

---

[1] *Jenseits von Gut und Böse,* VII, pp. 9, 56.
[2] *Ibid.,* p. 4.
[3] *Die Fröhliche Wissenschaft,* V, p. 252 ; *Jenseits von Gut und Böse,* VII, p. 12.
[4] *Jenseits von Gut und Böse,* VII, pp. 27, 33, 55–57.

after having brought the world into unity with mental processes, the latter can be shown to be derived from a single form of the will, the simplification will be complete. To accomplish this, one needs only to assume that all the impulses are merely different expressions of the will for power. The whole world, then, in its intellectual character is will for power and nothing else.[1]

Nietzsche's view of metaphysics is much the same as that described as belonging to the second period. In spite of the fact that he has himself advanced a definite metaphysical theory, he says that the only proper attitude is that of scepticism.[2] The philosophers of the future will be sceptics. It is the one justifiable position. Science is given little consideration, but the change of opinion with regard to it is more apparent than real. The supreme place, which it held during the intellectual period, is now accorded to philosophy as distinguished from metaphysics ; but the meaning of philosophy in the third period and of science in the second seems to be almost identical. The word science, on the other hand, has come to be applied to what was formerly designated as learning or professional knowledge.

The increase of radicalism in Nietzsche's position has strengthened it, so far as logical consistency goes. With the surrender of a hypothetical standard of truth, with which the historical errors could be somehow compared, the most obvious objection to his theory is annulled. The more fundamental inconsistency, however, still remains. How is it possible to carry through an argument, every step of which is determined by error? It is the old difficulty, which goes back to the beginnings of philosophy. If everything is denied, is not the denial itself included? Besides, if every theory has merely individual validity, why did Nietzsche attempt to defend his views, and why did he object so strongly, when people differed from him? It was rather hard to demand that all great minds should think exactly alike, and that for differences of opinion one must have recourse to the common herd. One may question, too, what is meant by the theory of the will for power.

[1] *Op. cit.*, p. 23.
[2] *Ibid.*, pp. 158–162 ; *Der Antichrist*, VIII, pp. 293–295.

Intellectual individualism seems to preclude the serious proposal of any general theory. It is all very well to urge that the doctrine regards the basal character of the universe as non-intellectual force, and so confirms the denial of a standard of truth; but in so far as the will for power is a theory, in as far as it enters into language or even into thought,—and apart from these it is nothing, at least for us,—in so far it has ceased to be blind force. A theory must be judged by intellectual standards. There is much to be said for the individualist's position; in a certain sense it is impossible to get beyond oneself and to find or use any other standard than that afforded by one's own mind; but such a position, if pushed to extremes, makes impossible any statement that is more than an expression of individual opinion. Perhaps Nietzsche would not have claimed a more general validity for his theories, and yet even the criterion of good taste must go back to some standard.

Sec. 2. Religion, Especially Christianity.

At first sight, Nietzsche's position with regard to religion and Christianity seems to have undergone no change, and to be essentially the same as that of the intellectual period. In reality, however, the only common factor is the unflinching opposition to both which he always maintains. The general attitude, which furnishes the motive for the opposition, has undergone a radical modification. The most scathing criticism to be made upon Christianity is no longer that it is not true, but that it is at once a symptom and a cause of degeneration. The emphasis has ceased to be placed upon intellectual errors, and now concerns practical influence upon action, and the development of personality. For the truly free spirits atheism is a necessity. God is a supposition; but no supposition should go further than the creative will can go, and no one can create a God.[1] There should be no gratuitous assumptions, none that cannot be joined to action, and made a source of power. Furthermore, no supposition should go beyond thought, and it is impossible to think God. One's own reason

---

[1] *Die fröhliche Wissenschaft*, V, p. 271; *Also sprach Zarathustra*, VI, pp. 123–125.

and will must create one's world, and the existence of God would leave nothing to create. ' If there were Gods, how could one endure not to be a God? Therefore there are no Gods.'

Historically there has always been belief in divinities. So long as a people has confidence in itself and in its own strength, it has its own God.[1] In him it honors the conditions of its own preservation, especially those of its own character. Such a God must be able to injure as well as to help. He must be not only a good friend, but a good enemy. His bad qualities are quite as prominent as his excellencies. It is not until the nation begins to degenerate that their God becomes merely a good God. The next step is to share him with other nations, to give him a cosmopolitan character. The pride of the race in itself is gone, and with it all the manly virtues of its God, who has become a divinity of the weak. If such a degenerated people is conquered by some stronger tribe, it takes revenge upon its masters by transforming their God into a devil, and the dualistic fiction of a good and a bad divinity is thus made complete.

The Christian concept of God is one of the most corrupt known,[2] and both the religion and the morality connected with it are utterly false.[3] Christianity deals entirely with imaginary quantities. It treats of such causes as God and the soul and is therefore fiction from beginning to end. The foremost place is given to the instincts of the lower classes.[4] As a means against tedium religion makes use of the casuistry of sin, of self-criticism. The highest is unattainable, save as a gift from God. The body is despised, hygiene ignored. Cruelty towards oneself and others is fostered, together with hatred of the rulers, of intellect, freedom, and the senses. Christianity has waged war to the death with the higher type of man, and has ruined the reason even of the mentally strong, by teaching that intellectuality is a sin.[5] It has continually taken the part of the weak, and has helped to preserve those who ought to have perished. It has taught sympathy, and so

[1] *Der Antichrist*, VIII, pp. 232, 233–235.
[2] *Morgenröte*, IV, pp. 86, 87.
[3] *Der Antichrist*, VIII, pp. 231, 232.
[4] *Ibid.*, pp. 238, 239.
[5] *Ibid.*, pp. 219–223.

has increased suffering and loss of strength.   It is an instrument
in the hands of the forces that make for degeneration.   In fact,
to be a Christian, one must be ill.[1]

The whole symbolism of Christianity is rude and in bad taste.[2]
It had to be adapted to the barbarian peoples which it wished to
influence.   What could be worse than the ceremony of the Lord's
Supper?   It must be admitted, however, that Christianity has
shown cleverness in using the means at its disposal.   The three
masterpieces are its doctrines of faith, hope, and love—faith in
something, no matter whether true or false, hope in another world,
and love for a God who has been given attributes various enough
to suit all ages and dispositions.

The spiritual father of Christianity is Judaism, with its denial
of everything favorable to-life.   At the beginning, Christianity
was a movement against the Jewish priestly caste.[3]   Jesus was
merely a criminal, and was punished for his misdeeds.   His doctrine was not a creed, but a special way of living, which perished
with him.   After his death, his disciples began to ask who killed
him; and in the spirit of revenge against the Jewish hierarchy,
the Christian church was established.[4]   Its founders, especially
Paul, falsified everything, even history.   They invented cunning
dogmas, by which all differences of caste were destroyed.   The
belief in the salvation of the soul really means that all the world
turns about the person in question.   Judge not, they said, but
they condemned to hell everything that stood in their way.[5]

Christianity destroyed all the labor of the ancient world.[6]   All
the presuppositions, including the method, for a learned culture
were present, but Christianity brought them to naught.   Later it
did the same thing for Islam, which was at least a religion for
men, not for slaves.   Last of all, it killed the Renaissance.

Sec. 3. Derivation of Morality.

In moral valuations there are two sets of opposites: good and
evil (*schlecht*), and good and bad (*böse*), and these have a different history.   The first pair, good and evil, express the valuations

[1] *Op. cit.*, pp. 287–291.
[2] *Ibid.*, pp. 237–242.
[3] *Ibid.*, pp. 249–251.
[4] *Ibid.*, pp. 267–273.
[5] *Ibid.*, p. 275.
[6] *Ibid.*, pp. 307–312.

of the ruling class in relation to their inferiors.[1] Here good, far from being a synonym for altruism, is rather the mark set upon the egoistic action *per se*. Whatever expresses the will of the individual is good. All that he does and is, his impulses, his passions, and his actions, everything that is a part of himself, he calls good. Whatever is different is to be scorned and despised ; it is evil. In the German language, for instance, *schlecht* is *schlicht*. The proof of this derivation of moral concepts is to be found in etymology. In all languages the first meaning of the word *good* is *noble, of high birth*.[2] It begins with expressing a class distinction, and is afterwards extended to mental and spiritual qualities. The aristocrats called themselves, on account of their superiority in power, lords and commanders ; but they also used names that designated some typical trait of character.[3] For instance, the Greek noblemen, as represented by Theognis, is called ἐσθλός. From its root, this means something that is, something that has reality, that is true, then, with a subjective application, the true in the sense of the truthful. · In the time of Theognis, the term belonged strictly to the nobility, and had become the equivalent for a man of rank. Truthfulness was one of the qualities that separated him from the common man, whom Theognis pictures as a liar. Finally, after the downfall of the nobility, the word came to mean the spiritually truthful, the nobleman in a moral sense. The opposite of ἀγαθός, κακός or δειλός, emphasizes cowardice, not wickedness.

In the Latin *malus* (connected with the Greek μέλας), the common man was called the dark-colored, especially the black-haired,—that is, he belonged to the pre-Arians, the original inhabitants of Italy, who were distinguished by their color from the ruling blood Arians. The Gaelic offers a like case. *Fin*, for instance, in the name Fin Gal, designated the noble, and later came to mean the good ; but originally it was the name for the blond conqueror in distinction from the dark, black-haired aboriginal. The Latin *bonus* is a warrior. *Bonus* or *duonus* has the

[1] *Zur Geneologie der Moral*, VII, pp. 303–305 ; *Jenseits von Gut und Böse*, VII, 239–243, 251, 252.

[2] *Zur Geneologie der Moral*, VII, pp. 306, 307.

[3] *Ibid.*, pp. 307–309.

same root as *bellum, duellum, duenlum;* that is, the good man was a fighter (*duo*). The German word *gut* probably means the godlike (*göttlich*), and is identical with the name given to the Goths.

In the same way, every designation of mental or spiritual superiority was at first a term indicative of political lordship. The fact that at times the highest caste was made up of priests, forms no exception to this rule.[1] In such a case, the masters naturally chose as descriptive of themselves words that savored of their priestly function. These, of course, are not to be regarded too symbolically. Pure means no more than the man who washes himself, who refrains from certain foods that cause skin diseases, who has no intercourse with the women of the lower class, and who has a dislike of blood. Such valuations are a source of danger, not to be apprehended from the rougher distinctions of the warrior. The priestly aristocracy always has something unhealthy in it, and often results in the neurasthenia, so common in the middle ages. The men of to-day are still suffering from the effects of the priestly caste; but one must not forget that they owe to it the fact that they have become interesting and bad, —the two advantages that man has over the animal. Whenever the priest and warrior meet, there is trouble.[2] The valuations of the latter presuppose health, with all the conditions necessary for its maintenance; that is to say, war, adventure, the hunt, the dance, combats, everything that requires strong and free action. The priests, on the contrary, since they lack this power and strength, hate it and all who possess it. The greatest and most intelligent hatreds in history have been on the part of priests. The best instance of the priestly caste is furnished by the Jews. Their hatred of the rulers and their revenge upon them took the form of a transvaluation of moral values. They put away the old aristocratic judgments of worth, and established in their stead entirely different ones. According to their ethics, only the poor are good; only the ill or ugly are pious; only those of low degree have a share in blessedness; while the noble and strong are

---

[1] *Ibid.*, pp. 309–311.
[2] *Ibid.*, pp. 312, 313; *Jenseits von Gut und Böse*, VII, pp. 126, 127.

godless, forever accursed and condemned. The instrument that the Jews used to make their revenge effective was Jesus of Nazareth.[1] With characteristic cunning they crucified him themselves, in order that the rest of the world might suspect nothing, and might thoughtlessly accept the ethical standards set up by his followers. To this trick is due the prevalence of the Christian morality, which, in spite of the fact that it is a poor thing, fit only for slaves, has nevertheless come to be almost everywhere predominant.

The Jews, however, were not the only discoverers or inventors of a slave morality. It is found wherever there is a resentment that cannot express itself in action.[2] Such a code of morality, in order to arise at all, must have opposition. It is essentially reaction and denial. The aristocratic morality, on the contrary, is above all an affirmation, which opposition only serves to make more pronounced. The opposition itself is of little weight as compared with the positive element. The latter expresses itself freely and simply without hatred or falsification. Its judgments are sometimes mistaken, but only concerning matters with which it is insufficiently acquainted. It often misunderstands the common man, to be sure; yet, the misunderstanding that is the result of scorn is never so great as that brought about by the hatred and revenge of the ignoble classes. The aristocrat takes the common man too lightly to change the object of his scorn into a caricature. His feeling is even not far removed from a careless sort of pity. Almost all the words applied by the Greek noble to the people, have in them some element expressive of unhappiness ($\delta\epsilon\iota\lambda\delta\varsigma$, $\delta\epsilon\iota\lambda\alpha\iota o\varsigma$, $\pi o\gamma\eta\rho\delta\varsigma$, $\mu o\chi\theta\eta\rho\delta\varsigma$). The well-born always feel that happiness is their own prerogative, and moreover that it is something positive in its nature, which does not need to be artificially constructed, by means of a comparison of their own condition with that of other men. They scarcely separate happiness from action ($\epsilon\check{\upsilon}$ $\pi\rho\dot{\alpha}\tau\tau\epsilon\iota\nu$). With the common people on the other hand, happiness has nothing to do with action. All that they desire is passive rest and peace. As the slavish caste,

---

[1] *Zur Geneologie der Moral,* VII, pp. 314, 315.
[2] *Ibid.,* pp. 317–320.

they always keep their eyes on their superiors, and measure everything through its relation to their rulers. There is nothing open and honorable about their actions and ideas; they are not strong enough to defend themselves, except by means of fraud, and everything twisted and false is regarded as a means of safety. Naturally, then, the common man becomes cleverer than the noble. With the one cleverness is a condition of existence, while to the other it is little more than a luxury. The aristocrat can afford to be defrauded sometimes. As for enemies, he could not exist without them, and he wants one worthy of his steel. The common man, on the contrary, being too weak and too cowardly to fight, regards an enemy as wicked. To him bad does not mean despicable, but dangerous.

Evil and bad, though of such different origin, are both looked upon as the opposite of good, but the latter concept does not keep the same meaning in the two cases.[1] With the aristocrats, good is the positive term, and evil is merely absence of good. Every form of self-expression is praiseworthy, no matter how much it transgresses every moral precept of the vulgar code. The nobleman, however strongly he may be bound by custom, reverence, or gratitude to his equals, feels none of these trammels in his intercourse with men of a lower class. At bottom he is little better than a savage, and every freedom from social compulsion gives him pleasure. He is the "blond beast," eager for booty and victory. He must go back at times to the wilderness, where he can display the animal part of his nature. He delights in destruction and in cruelty. Evidently, this unrestrained freedom, which is called good by the ruling class, is branded by the slaves as bad. It forms the positive element in their morality, and for them good is merely its negation. The whole progress of culture has been to destroy the aristocratic ideal in favor of the slavish one. The man of to-day is despicable in his pettiness; the "blond beast" has become a house animal. There is no moral advance in this change. To demand of the strong that he should not manifest his strength, is just as absurd as to ask the weak suddenly to become strong.[2] Strength is merely the im-

---

[1] *Op. cit.*, pp. 321–325; *Jenseits von Gut und Böse*, VII, p. 127.
[2] *Zur Geneologie der Moral*, VII, pp. 326–334.

pulse and the power to act in a certain way. The lower classes make the mistake of supposing that both their rulers and themselves freely chose their own course of conduct. They look upon strength as a vice, and count their weakness as the greatest of virtues, oblivious of the fact that both qualities are the inevitable adjuncts of certain types of character. They say to themselves : " Let us be different from our wicked rulers, let us be good. The good man is he who uses no violence, who injures no one, who leaves revenge to God, who demands little from life, in short, one who lives exactly as we do." According to their definition, the weak are good, if they see the virtuous nature of their condition and attempt nothing too hard for them.

The two opposing systems have had a terrible struggle, and although, on the whole, the slave-morality has long been more powerful, there are places where the conflict is not yet decided.[1] Rome and Judea are typical of the two. The last great victory of the Jewish ideal took place in the French Revolution, where it conquered the only aristocracy remaining in Europe, the French nobility of the seventeenth and eighteenth centuries. This was followed, however, by the rise of Napoleon, the noble ideal incarnate, who, in his turn, was done to death by the slaves.

There is no need to define the morality of Europe to-day. It is evidently that of the slaves. It glorifies everything that is useful to the common people.[2] Long habit has brought about an instinct for obedience, which satisfies itself at the expense of the nobler art of command. If the men of to-day are obliged to rule, they do it with a half-concealed remorse, or else they try to convince themselves that they are merely stewards, who are carrying out the commands of a higher power. They emphasize the value of everything that tends to make the common lot easier, for instance, sympathy, patience, industry, modesty and friendliness.[3] In their valuations and in their actions they are slaves.

Evidently this account of the origin and growth of the two opposing systems of morality is different from anything found in the

---

[1] *Op. cit.*, pp. 334–337 ; *Jenseits von Gut und Böse*, VII, p. 131.

[2] *Jenseits von Gut und Böse*, VII, pp. 129–134.

[3] *Ibid.*, pp. 239–243.

second period.   Nietzsche himself affirms that he stated essentially the same position in *Menschliches allzu Menschliches ;* [1] but there, although the aristocrat- and the slave-morality are briefly described, the latter is declared to be necessarily self-destructive ; and the moral standards of the present time are derived from the valuations of the ruling classes. [2]   The objections to the theory in its present form fall into two groups : (1) those which relate to its intrinsic probability ; and (2) those referring to the specific historical and etymological proofs.   The latter may be conveniently discussed first.   The statement that the concept *good* always goes back to that of noble birth has been denied, although such a connection is not difficult to establish for the Greek language.   This, however, cannot be regarded as corroborative of Nietzsche's theory, unless it can be shown that the gradual change in the meaning of the word *good* was the result of an increase of slavish influence.   There seems to be no ground for such an assumption.   During the second half of the fifth century, when the aristocratic power of both Athens and Sparta was at its height, the meanings *good* in birth and *good* in morals were used interchangeably.   Moreover, some of the specific etymologies given by Nietzsche have been disputed. [3]   According to Riehl, these derivations had already been published in Paul Rée's book, *Die Entstehung des Gewissens*, where references were made to P. E. Müller, Grote and Welcker. [4]   But, as Lichtenberger points out, the theory does not necessarily stand or fall with the etymologies.

The one instance cited by Nietzsche of the victory of a slave-morality, is that brought about by the Jews in Christianity.   The question is not as to the essential characteristics of Christian ethics, but concerns merely the credibility of the statement that the Jews deliberately, in a spirit of revenge, imposed it on their conquerors.   As a matter of history, the thing is too absurd to be discussed seriously.   One would be almost disposed to think that one had mistaken Nietzsche's meaning, if he had not been

[1] *Zur Geneologie der Moral*, VII, p. 288.

[2] II, pp. 68, 69.

[3] C. C. Everett, *Beyond Good and Evil, The New World*, Dec., '98, p. 690.

[4] *Friedrich Nietzsche, Der Künstler und der Denker*, p. 109.

so explicit, and if the numerous commentators upon his work were not practically at one upon the matter.

Viewing the question entirely apart from its historical aspect, one must admit that Nietszsche is right in saying that different conditions result in different moral standards. The form of the concepts may remain the same, but their content will differ. The man accustomed to command does not take the day laborer's views of humanity. Caste distinctions and the varying degrees of culture that usually accompany them, bring about an infinite series of moral judgments, some of which are the exact opposites of others. The parallelism between conditions and ethical valuations is so close, however, it is carried out to such fine gradations, that any attempt to divide the varying standards into two great classes would be only an abstraction. As such, it might have a value for classification, but otherwise would be of little use. The morality of the present is doubtless a compound of many moralities, but one must admit that Nietzsche has not furnished adequate proof of the special derivation that he advocates. It remains an assumption.

Sec. 4. Responsibility and Punishment.

The primitive idea of punishment is that everything has its equivalent and can be paid for.[1] There is the same relation between injury and subsequent pain as there is between a debt and its payment. The original contract in the latter case was somewhat as follows. The debtor gave some surety, so that, in case he could not pay, the creditor had a right to his wife, or his freedom, or his life. There was an equivalent between money or land on the one side, and the pleasure of inflicting pain on the other. The lower the creditor stood in the social scale, the more he delighted in exercising cruelty, for he thereby gained a taste of the pleasures belonging to a higher order. The people delighted in cruelty. In fact, the revolting thing about suffering is not the pain itself, but the thought that it exists without a reason. The remedy offered by Christianity was to make pain a part of the secret machinery of salvation. The ancients accomplished

[1] *Zur Geneologie der Moral*, VII, pp. 350–364.

the same end by providing pleased onlookers. If these were lacking in the flesh, the gods took their places, and were supposed to take the same delight in the spectacle.

The commonwealth stands in a like relation to its members as the creditor to the debtor. The criminal is the man who has broken his compact with the whole. He is given back to the pre-social conditions, and every sort of hostility is let loose upon him. As the state increases in power, the transgressions of the individual become less dangerous, and therefore are not taken so seriously. The universal anger may no longer vent itself without restraint upon the evil-doer, but he is protected by the state. Every injury has its price, and a compromise is made with the injured party ; that is, the criminal and his deed are to a certain extent separated. It is possible to conceive of such an increase of power that punishment would be altogether destroyed. Justice would then annul itself.

In considering the origin and end of punishment, one must remember that the two are different.[1] The uses to which a thing is put are continually changing. In the beginning, punishment utilized some procedure already existing, and put it to a different use. An accurate definition of punishment is now impossible, because in the course of development it has meant so many contradictory things, all of which have contributed to its present meaning. For instance, punishment has been thought of as a hindrance to further injury, as an adjustment of the advantages that the criminal had previously enjoyed, as a festival, as a compromise with natural revenge. A supposed utility of punishment is the awakening of the feeling of guilt in the criminal, but that is precisely what it does not do. Among such classes the stings of conscience are rare. In fact, in the past punishment has hindered the development of the feeling of guilt. The criminal saw that his judges made use of the same sort of actions that they condemned in him. For a long time he said merely that he ought to have been more clever ; punishment made him more careful, but not better.

The stings of conscience are the result of a fundamental change

[1] *Op. cit.*, pp. 369–385.

in the life of a man who has hitherto been free to carry on war and adventure. Suddenly he finds himself in the bonds of society, while all his instincts are still adapted to the wilderness. Denied their customary satisfaction, they turn against their owner. The pleasure in cruelty and persecution, which was once exercised against others, is now given free scope upon himself, and he becomes a prey to the feeling of guilt and all its attendant horrors. Of course, this theory presupposes that the change is sudden and involuntary, yet so complete that there is no opportunity for defence nor even for resentment. It presupposes too, that the adaptations to the new circumstances, begun with force, are necessarily carried on by like means. The same instincts are present in both conquerors and conquered, but in the latter they are denied their natural outlet, and so give rise to the stings of conscience.

Sec. 5., The Moral Ideal.—Fullness of Life versus Degeneration.

The most fundamental characteristic of degeneration is the weakening of the will. It is essentially a denial of life, a pessimism that takes refuge in inactivity. The instincts that are powerful in the healthy organism, and that lead it to support itself at the expense of others, are not only absent, but are even despised and shunned. This is, unfortunately, the condition of the present age. There is a trace of illness everywhere. Virtue is petty, vice is anæmic. Nowhere is there enough force to accomplish anything either good or bad. Life is an instinct for growth and permanence, but the modern ideals all point away from this goal.[1] The so-called higher feelings are really preferences for what is injurious. They call upon men to work and think without the sanction of pleasure.[2] They leave out the personal element altogether and put an abstraction in its stead. This problem of decadence is most important, so much so that the question of good and evil is only its sportive side, so to speak.[3] One cannot get away from its influence into an entirely healthy atmosphere. Nietzsche admits that he is a child of his time, and so a degenerate. He

[1] *Der Antichrist*, VIII, pp. 220, 221.
[2] *Ibid.*, pp. 226, 227.
[3] *Der Fall Wagner*, VIII, p. 1.

possesses one advantage over the others, however ; he recognizes
his condition and so is enabled to fight against it.

All judgments of the worth of life, whether positive or negative, are symptoms of the state of health of the men who make
them.[1] In themselves they are of no value, because, while a
man lives, he cannot get far enough away from life to form an
adequate judgment of it. That the wise men of all times have
agreed in regarding life as worthless, proves nothing with respect
to life, but shows merely that these wise men were degenerates.
The spiritualization of the senses, the softening of everything
harsh and hard, is one of the contributions of Christianity to the
progress of degeneration.[2] The true morality, that of nature, re-
joices in opposition. It requires enemies. The desire for peace
comes only with age ; and while health and strength last, the
one demand is for complete affirmation of life. One of the necessities for the development of such characteristics is continual
conflict of some kind.[3] A good war sanctifies every cause.
Courage is one of the cardinal virtues, while cowardice is despicable. One should fear neither oneself nor others, neither
suffering nor combat. The true man takes pleasure in strife.
Nothing would suit him less than the comfortable peace that is
concerned only with maintaining an even temperature and avoiding all trouble.

In fact, at the bottom of everything lies the will for power.[4]
Strength and force and joy in using them are the foremost qualities of the higher man. Cesare Borgia had the quality to an
unusual degree, for in him it had not degenerated into weakness
and virtue. Self-assertion is the first and last command.[5] Life
is essentially the overcoming of the foreign and the weak. It is
worse than nonsense to restrain such impulses ; without them
life would be an impossibility. The better way is to give them
full play, and rejoice in the strength that fears nothing, but rather

---

[1] *Götzendämmerung*, VIII, pp. 68, 88.

[2] *Ibid.*, pp. 84, 85.

[3] *Also sprach Zarathustra*, VI, pp. 66–68.

[4] *Götzendämmerung*, VIII, pp. 123, 124, 127, 128, 145–148 ; *Die fröhliche Wissenschaft*, V, pp. 41, 50.

[5] *Jenseits von Gut und Böse*, VII, pp. 237, 238.

seeks out the terrible and demands a great enemy.[1] Such an ideal may be called immoral; but is it really so?[2] All ages have tried to improve man, and have succeeded only in making him weaker. The animals in a menagerie have been made less dangerous, but are they better? Is there not something despicable in a self-denial that means only restraint? Everything is good that increases the will to power;[3] everything is evil that springs from weakness,—not satisfaction but more power; not peace but war; not virtue but ability.

The strong man is proud. If he cannot live proudly he will die proudly;[4] and the best death is that willed by the self.[5] He delights in solitude; he can stand alone.[6] He is dependent on no one, not even on the person whom he loves best. He clings to no country, not even to one in need of help. He has freed himself from everything, sympathy, science, his own virtues. He is bound at no point, but is the most perfect expression of the free will, with all its caprices and whims. He is no altruist.[7] His instincts are too healthy for that. Unegoistic morality is an offence against good taste.[8] To desire or show sympathy is unmanly.[9] God died of sympathy, and it was Zarathustra's last sin. Where it is preached there is always an echo of self-scorn. Suffering should be increased, not diminished. Only the discipline of great pain brings elevation; the hard, the difficult is holy. Besides, sympathy displays a lack of delicacy, it hurts the pride of others. It is cruel to look at another's pain as sympathy does. Healthy egoism confines its attention to itself, except when it is conquering an enemy.[10] One must learn

[1] *Menschliches allzu Menschliches*, III, p. 11 (*Vorrede*, written in 1886); *Götzendämmerung*, VIII, pp. 149, 150.

[2] *Götzendämmerung*, VIII, pp. 102, 103.

[3] *Der Antichrist*, VIII, p. 218.

[4] *Götzendämmerung*, VIII, pp. 143–145.

[5] *Also sprach Zarathustra*, VII, p. 105–108.

[6] *Also sprach Zarathustra*, VII, pp. 73–77. *Jenseits von Gut und Böse*, VII, pp. 61, 62.

[7] *Morgenröte*, IV, p. 151; *Götzendämmerung*, VIII, pp. 142, 143.

[8] *Jenseits von Gut und Böse*, VII, pp. 174, 175, 269, 270.

[9] *Also sprach Zarathustra*, VI, pp. 84, 128, 130, 351; *Jenseits von Gut und Böse*, VII, pp. 175, 179–181; *Götzendämmerung*, VIII, pp. 89, 90.

[10] *Ibid.*, p. 282, 298, 318..

to love oneself with an undivided love ; one should be happy, and scorn the world. It is naïveté to pretend that man should be other than he is, to arrogate to oneself the right to say what he ought to be.

Such a morality must necessarily be confined to the few, and Nietzsche nowhere advocates its adoption by any but the rare exceptions. The common people may struggle along as they can. There is not much in life for them at best. They exist only for the sake of their masters. If they contribute a little to the support of the favored aristocrats, they should count themselves happy ; or rather, since they cannot be expected to appreciate so elevated a morality, that is all that their lords will demand of them. The great objection to such an arrangement is that it makes all organized society impossible. If every man's hand is against every man, the most primitive conditions of culture must prevail. Even with a well-disciplined lower class, the constant war of the few, since they have all the power, must mean anarchy. To be sure, there are an abundance of people who assert that that is precisely Nietzsche's social ideal. Yet an anarchy that permits individual development must be of a somewhat subdued nature, and Nietzsche always emphasizes the importance of personality. Without a more detailed account than he offers of the way in which both elements may be given free scope, it is difficult to see how they can exist together. Each seems destined to make the other impossible.

It is a mistake, however, to accuse Nietzsche of having destroyed all moral valuations. He has set up different ones from those generally accepted, that is all. There is no attempt to dispense with a standard altogether. As he himself says, *Jenseits von Gut und Böse* does not mean *Jenseits von Gut und Schlecht*.[1] It is the reëstablishment of the aristocrat morality in place of the slavish standard of Christianity, an invitation to go back to the good old days of the noble savage.

Sec. 6. The Over-man and the Eternal Recurrence.

Even Nietzsche was unable to do without some kind of moral ideal, something to be striven for which would justify all life.

[1] *Zur Geneologie der Moral*, VII, pp. 337, 338.

He found this in the Over-man, the end and aim of all existence. Doubtless the prevalent evolutionary theories of the time had more or less influence upon the formation of this ideal, but it must not be confused with the ordinary development theories which consider an elevation of the human type a possibility. Mankind as a whole, according to Nietzsche, is not advancing but deteriorating.[1] The European of to-day is inferior to his ancestors of the Renaissance age. The Over-man seems to be rather a mystical product of the individual will, though his exact nature is veiled in obscurity.[2] Whether he represents an ideal that will one day be attained by the higher type of man as a whole, or whether he is the goal set for the development of each aristocrat in and for himself, is uncertain. The weight of evidence seems to be equally divided between the two suppositions. Perhaps the simplest interpretation is that the ideal, though at present unattainable by the higher man, should be nevertheless the object of his life ; and since a race or a type is no more than a collection of individuals, every approach to the goal on the part of the single aristocrat lifts the entire class so much the nearer.

The most striking thing about the entire doctrine is its affirmation of all that makes for life. Negation has no place there. No degenerate need expect to advance toward the Over-man. Schopenhauer's ideal man, with his denial of the will to live, could never reach it. Yet the part played by the Over-man in Nietzsche's philosophy is much the same as that of the saint in Schopenhauer's. In both, the ideal is held up as the end and aim of life, as its only meaning, worthy of the greatest conceivable sacrifice. The Over-man is proclaimed with all the fervor of a religious enthusiast, with all the eager earnestness of a fanatic.

[1] *Der Antichrist*, VIII, p. 219.

[2] *Jenseits von Gut und Böse*, VII, pp. 137–139. Peter Gast, in his preface to the second edition of *Also sprach Zarathustra*, says that the Over-man is a symbol. An individual can have a part in the Over-man, but cannot be one. There seems to be no justification for this view. Lichtenberger defines the Over-man as follows : " the state to which man will attain, when he has renounced the existing hierarchy of values, the Christian ideal, democratic or ascetic, that is current to-day in the whole of modern Europe, and has returned to the table of values acknowledged among the noble races, among the masters, who themselves create the values that they recognize, instead of receiving them from without." (*La Philosophie de Nietzsche*, p. 149.)

It is not a philosophical theory to be proven, but a saving doctrine to be unquestioningly accepted by every devout aristocrat.

The Over-man, though mentioned in several of Nietzsche's later books, is discussed most fully in the prose poem, *Also sprach Zarathustra*. The allegorical nature of this work and the mystical way in which the story is written, render interpretation difficult. As a result, while some writers regard the central figure, Zarathustra, as a picture of the Over-man, others see in him only the forerunner and prophet. He preaches the Over-man, and longs for the coming that he is not destined to see. On the whole, the second interpretation seems to have more to recommend it, but the question is not of much importance. In either case Zarathustra is an ideal, and whether he himself represents the final goal of human development, or only an intermediate stage, the doctrines that he preaches remain the same.

These doctrines are, on the whole, identical with those advocated in the other books of this period. The present man is something to be overcome, to be left behind, as unworthy of further notice.[1] His only value is that he may be made a bridge to the Over-man. As the ape is to the man, so will the man be to the Over-man. The task of each individual is to learn to acquiesce in the necessary self-destruction. He must not only realize that the Over-man expresses the meaning of the world, but he must rejoice in the existence of such a meaning. Mere submission is not sufficient. What is needed is the strength to will that the Over-man shall come, and the man perish. The road to this affirmation is not through scorn of the earth nor of the body.[2] To despise what is called matter is no way to the Over-man. Now that God is dead, the greatest sin is that against the earth.

One of the requisites for whoever would help to bring about the coming of the Over-man is an attitude of complete scepticism with regard to all that claims admiration. Everything must be questioned, especially the various forms of self-satisfaction. Even the virtues are not exempt from the general condemnation.

[1] *Also sprach Zarathustra*, VI, pp. 13–15.
[2] *Ibid.*, p. 48.

All virtue is an earthly virtue, and wills self-destruction. He who protects his neighbor delays the coming of the Over-man.[1] One must will the destruction of the individual, in order that the Over-man may live.

Closely connected with this doctrine is that of the eternal recurrence. Zarathustra proclaims that this life, with all its qualities and situations and people, is only a part of an endless cycle which is continually repeating itself.[2] Has not all that can happen already happened; and must it not happen again? Even to the smallest details everything will repeat itself, just as it has a countless number of times in the past. The same causes must always have the same results, and no new elements are ever introduced. The same combinations take place over and over. As Zarathustra says: "I see this doorway has two faces,—two ways come together here; no one has ever travelled them to the end. This long alley goes back for an eternity, and that one goes on,—that is another eternity. The name of the doorway is a moment. Must not everything that can go already have gone down this path? Must not everything that could happen already have happened, and this slow spider that crawls in the moonlight, and this moonlight itself, and I and thou and the doorway, whispering together, whispering of eternal things,— must we not all have been here already, and come back, and gone on into that other path? Must we not eternally come back?"

This half-mystic doctrine was accepted by Nietzsche only after a long struggle. His life had been so unhappy that he could not endure to think of living it again. At first he dreaded the theory, treating it less as a conviction than as a fear.[3] He thought that a scientific basis and proof might be found for it in the theories of the atomists; and in the summer of 1882 he decided to cease all literary work for ten years, and to devote that time to the study of science at Paris, Vienna, or Munich.[4] Illness

---

[1] *Ibid.*, p. 291.

[2] *Nietzsche contra Wagner*, VIII, p. 174; *Also sprach Zarathustra*, VI, pp. 232, 321.

[3] Frau Lou Andreas-Salomé, *Friedrich Nietzsche in seinen Werken*, pp. 222–224.

[4] *Ibid.*, pp. 141, 142.

prevented him from carrying out this plan, and he gradually
came to see that science had nothing to say upon the subject of
eternal recurrence.   Once freed from the burden of proclaiming
an unrecognized scientific truth, his dread of the theory lessened.[1]
It even came to be a favorite of his, and to take on something of
the religious nature with which he clothed that other theory of
the Over-man.   Its significance for the system lies entirely, according to Professor Seth, in its relation to life.[2]   The supreme
act of will is shown in the joyous acceptance of the most adverse
conditions.   When a man realizes that the worst suffering is
nothing as compared with his own powers of endurance, he
dreads no destiny, even though he knows that he must undergo
it a countless number of times.   Like Milton's Lucifer, his pride
makes him a match for fate.[3]

Also sprach Zarathustra is the story of the prophet and priest
of these mysteries.   A solitary dweller upon a lonely mountain,
with an eagle and a serpent for his only companions, he found
his own wisdom a burden, and he longed to impart it to others.
So he returned to the valley and wandered about, preaching the
life of the instincts and the sanctity of the earth.   The four parts
of the book are filled with his teachings, and with the account of
the distrust with which he was received, the manner in which he
gradually found disciples, and of his repeated returns to the
mountain, when solitude became a necessity either for him or for
his doctrines.   From the beginning he proclaimed the Over-
man, but the Eternal Recurrence was revealed to him gradually,
and he accepted it only after much reluctance.   The dread of the
doctrine shown in *Also sprach Zarathustra*, so closely parallel to
the history of Nietzsche's own feelings with regard to it, is one of
the reasons why so many commentators identify Zarathustra
with Nietzsche himself, and speak of Nietzsche-Zarathustra.

[1] *Ibid.*, pp. 224, 225.   Practically the same theory is found in Blanqui's *L' Eter-
nité par les Astres*, and also in Gustave Le Bon's *L' Homme et les Sociétés*.   The first
was published in 1871, the second in 1882.   According to Lichtenberger (*La Philosophie de Nietzsche*, pp. 185–189) there is not the slightest evidence to show that
Nietzsche was acquainted with the work of either of these men.

[2] *The Opinions of Friedrich Nietzsche, The Critical Review*, May, p. 735.

[3] *Ibid.*, p. 736.

There have been several attempts to explain the allegory in
Also sprach Zarathustra.   The most elaborate, as well as the
best, is that given by Lichtenberger.[1]   Neither explanation nor
allegory need concern us here.   Both are interesting, and the
story itself has a peculiar charm, due as much, perhaps, to its
style as to its content ; but it offers little that is new.   It is a
poetical presentation of Nietzsche's theories, rather than any addition to the accounts found in the other books.   Zarathustra is
the incarnation of Nietzsche's philosophy.   He furnishes it with
the æsthetic surroundings so suited to its nature, and makes it
vital, human.

[1] *La Philosophie de Nietzsche*, pp. 146–168 ; *Friedrich Nietzsche, Aphorismes et
Fragments Choisis*, pp. 41–45, 55–60, 69–75, 81–85, 94–102.

CHAPTER V.

NIETZSCHE'S RELATION TO OTHER WRITERS AND HIS SIGNIFICANCE.

Sec. 1. Schopenhauer.

It is generally agreed that, at the beginning of Nietzsche's career as a writer, he was a follower of Schopenhauer. His early work shows abundant traces of this influence, and though the writings of the later periods are much freer from such indications, one may well doubt whether even here the influence of Schopenhauer is entirely absent. There are not many definite theories that can be traced to the great pessimist, but without his work that of Nietzsche would have been impossible. A man's position often owes as much to what he opposes as to that with which he agrees, and some of Nietzsche's most characteristic doctrines originated in his opposition to Schopenhauer.

The lack of agreement between the two men would doubtless have been more striking, if they had not concerned themselves with such different problems. Schopenhauer was a metaphysician, a philosopher busied with discovering the ultimate nature of the universe, a follower of Plato and Kant. For him the term *Ding-an-sich* had not lost its profound meaning ; he still believed in a world-wide distinction between phenomenon and noumenon. Nietzsche, on the other hand, flung metaphysics to the winds. To be sure, he occasionally found difficulty in dispensing with it altogether, for metaphysics is like the law of contradiction. A man may refuse to accept it, but he constantly finds himself obliged to make use of it, if merely as an implicit basis. Nevertheless, Nietzsche did all that could be done, and discarded metaphysics so far as was possible. He deliberately turned away, not only from the tentative answers already given to its problems, but even from the problems themselves, and refused to consider such unsubstantial relations. For him the burning questions were those of personality, of life as it is lived, not as it is thought. Perhaps the circumstances of his own life, on the whole so uneventful and so withdrawn from activity, made him magnify the part played by physical energy in the world. To identify existence with man and to measure both by their effects is not the exclusive prerogative of the actor, but is often found in the onlooker as well. Not the soldier, but the man who merely dreams of war, deifies the power of the sword.

Although approaching the matter from such a different standpoint, Nietzsche fully agreed with Schopenhauer in regarding the will as logically prior to the intellect. In fact, during the first period he held practically Schopenhauer's view with regard to the relation between the will and the idea. Like most men, he began his life as thinker with a set of ready-made opinions, and without subjecting them overmuch to criticism, held them until he had become advanced enough to substitute for them more independent ones of his own. It was in this rôle of disciple that Nietzsche committed himself to most of the Schopenhauerian metaphysics. Among the notebooks since published by his sister, those which date from the time of *Die Geburt der Tragödie* and *Unzeitgemässe Betrachtungen* contain elaborate, though fragmentary, discussions of the essence of the universe and its dual nature as will and as idea.[1] The will is the *Ding-an-sich*, and the idea merely its phenomenal manifestation. Nietzsche differed from Schopenhauer, however, in making a distinction between conscious and unconscious idea.[2] Individuation is the result of the latter, of the universal ideating principle which through its longing for existence brings about the particular phenomena. Conscious ideation has nothing to do with the matter. This difference, however, is far from being fundamental, and had absolutely no influence in determining Nietzsche's position upon other matters.

It may be urged that all this is metaphysics, and that an attempt has been made to show that Nietzsche was not a metaphysician. It must be remembered, however, that he deliberately refrained from publishing these theories; and though they undoubtedly formed the basis of the æsthetics in *Die Geburt der*

[1] IX, pp. 47, 66, 67, 69–72, 130, 164–174.
[2] *Ibid.*, pp. 66, 67.

Tragödie, yet they may be almost likened to his philological equipment, and regarded as one of the tools with which he worked.   As his own theories developed, he threw aside whatever was extraneous to them, but held with all the greater tenacity to the kernel of the whole, the primacy of the will.[1] This became the central point of his own system in its most independent form, and here Schopenhauer's influence survived most strongly.   To be sure, the will to live has become the will for power, but it is still the will.   The idea has lost ground rather than gained it.

There has been some difference of opinion as to how closely one is justified in identifying the will for power with the will to live.   That they are not synonymous terms is evident, but neither are they to be regarded as opposites.   Whether the one is to be looked upon as a real advance upon the other, is a matter of interpretation, not only of Nietzsche but of Schopenhauer.   If the will to live is confined to bare existence, while the will for power is viewed in the most comprehensive light possible, he two are evidently far apart.   In comparison with the latter, Schopenhauer's motive principle seems almost passive.   Yet it may be doubted whether the will to live ever concerns bare existence, or even whether existence is possible without power. To will to live means to will to overcome other beings desirous of occupying the same place.   The theories differ only in degree. On the other hand, it is a mistake to emphasize overmuch the resemblance between them; and the golden mean that gives due importance to both likeness and diversity is hard to find.

Any system that centers itself in the will must cut loose more or less entirely from the traditional relation between logic and feeling.   If intellect is secondary, its rules no longer form a court of appeal before which everything must be brought for final confirmation or rejection.   Impulse gains a dignity hitherto unaccorded to it, at least in staid philosophical schools.   In his ethics Schopenhauer recognized fully the new position given to

---

[1] Nietzsche did not work out an elaborate system of gradations of manifestation of the will, nor did he attempt to prove his assumption of its universal nature, as Schopenhauer did in *Ueber den Willen in der Natur*.

feeling in all its guises, but Nietzsche went a step further. He saw that the change in the importance of feeling must not be limited to the domain of morality; that, if the will is supreme, feeling which furnishes its motive, and impulse which is a form either of feeling or of will, according to the point of view, are both superior to reason. Here again he followed in his master's footsteps, but at the same time went beyond the point gained by his predecessor.

In their attitudes toward life, Nietzsche and Schopenhauer are both reckoned among the pessimists; but any classificatory term so general in its significance is apt to be misleading, and in reality in this respect they stood far apart. Schopenhauer was a pessimist worthy of the name. In all the universe he found no single ray of hope. The future differed from the past only in being still more dreary, if there could be degrees in such a dead level of gloom. The result was quietism. Nothing is, nothing can ever be worth while. The only happiness for man is to cease to live. The very struggle to preserve such a wretched existence is a sin, nay, it is the source of the wretchedness itself. For the individual and so for the race the only justifiable goal is speedy annihilation.

Nietzsche accepted Schopenhauer's premises, but not his conclusions. He agreed at all times that the world was as bad as it could possibly be, that there was no help for it, and that optimism was either ignorance or superficiality. Nevertheless, he was no quietist. He could not understand the pride that accepts the inevitable in silence without a struggle. His own pride, though no less great, was that of the fighter. Fate is inexorable; true, but one can always defy it. Hardship and suffering are bound to overcome everyone, but the hero meets pain and despair with scorn. There is nothing to live for, perhaps, but he is strong enough to endure even that. In any case, opposition is abundant, and one can always fight.

Whether such a position is as consistent as Schopenhauer's is open to serious question. It implies that, though the amount of happiness does not justify life, yet the struggle and even the suffering make it worth while. The man who sets his teeth and challenges the universe may not be happy, but he has won something better than annihilation, and thereby renders any thorough-going pessimism an impossibility. Indeed, Nietzsche himself came to discard the term, and to adopt the alternative that he had himself proposed in the first period, namely, tragic optimism. With all the force of his strong nature he fought against quietism. That such an attitude is inconsistent with pessimism, is indicated by his constant endeavor to find some worthy end in the midst of the general aimlessness, some justification for life in spite of its evil. This attempt, tentative at first, gained in sureness and precision as he advanced. In the beginning, all he could find was a refuge in art, a flight from life itself to dreams of life. Later, he refused to turn his back upon suffering, and step by step he went on to a conception of the nobility of a true aristocracy, until with his Over-man he reached a moral, almost a religious justification of existence. He may have accepted the pessimistic formulas, but in reality he was not of that faith. To call him an optimist seems absurd; and yet, if one attempts a dichotomy, that is where he belongs. His optimism was severe of aspect. It knew little of happiness and still less of freedom from suffering. It glorified pain, even wickedness, and found its triumph in a joyous acceptance of evil.

With regard to specific theories, Schopenhauer had little lasting influence upon Nietzsche. Their interests were on the whole different, and wherever they touched by chance upon the same subjects, they seldom agreed, save in questions concerning æsthetics. One of the most striking of these disagreements was with regard to the value of truth. Nietzsche thought that not only progress, but the development of the human reason, art, culture, morality, everything worth while, in fact, was inevitably bound up with error. Schopenhauer, on the contrary, regarded truth and truth alone as in the end advantageous. "Every error," he says, "carries a poison within it."[1]

Even more fundamental, however, is the different attitude of the two men with regard to sympathy, and here Nietzsche undoubtedly found his starting point in a thorough-going opposi-

---

[1] *Die Welt als Wille und Vorstellung*, I, sec. 8.

tion to his master. Schopenhauer made sympathy the basis of all ethics. In a world of misery the chief virtue is to pity the suffering of one's fellow-victims and try to relieve them. This view was so repugnant to Nietzsche, he opposed it so vigorously, that he often speaks as if it were almost universal in ethical treatises.[1] Such a conception is evidently false, but perhaps Nietzsche seemed to hold it, only because of the ardor of his opposition.

In fact, as has already been hinted, Nietzsche was in complete agreement with Schopenhauer only in the field of æsthetics. In the *Geburt* he presupposed Schopenhauer's standpoint ; and, his two æsthetic principles, symbolized by Dionysus and Apollo, have been identified with Schopenhauer's *Wille* and *Vorstellung*. The comparison seems hardly justifiable, however, for the Dionysian element is the more direct manifestation of the will rather than the will itself. The distinction between the Apollinic and the Dionysian corresponds more exactly to Schopenhauer's division of the arts into two classes, one embracing all the descriptive, pictorial, and plastic arts, and the other reserved exclusively for music. Nietzsche made no attempt to apply his principle to the world as a whole. He was concerned simply with the æsthetic aspect, and though as an artist he was disposed to give this an overwhelming importance, yet it is a gratuitous assumption to suppose, without further evidence, that he extended the æsthetic classification to all conscious and unconscious existence. The position that he gave to music is exactly that of Schopenhauer.[2] They both considered music the highest form of art, in that it was the direct expression of the will without any intermediate stages.

Perhaps the reverence shown by Nietzsche for Schopenhauer's theories of art was partly due to the fact that Wagner accepted them no less devoutly. The three held essentially the same ideal of culture, in that they turned away from authority and placed the greatest emphasis upon the development of individuality. Schopenhauer and Nietzsche both preached the cult of

[1] Cf. Riehl : *Friedrich Nietzsche, Der Künstler und der Denker*, p. 86.
[2] *Die Welt als Wille und Vorstellung*, I, sec. 52.

genius, and the necessity of the most complete sacrifices, if one would aid in its production; but in their definition of genius they again differed. Schopenhauer found its essence to consist in the denial of the will, while, for Nietzsche, it was affirmation carried to the highest point.

On the whole, then, the likenesses between the two seem approximately equalled by the differences. The special praise given to Schopenhauer in Nietzsche's writings relates nearly always to his ideal of culture. What especially appealed to Nietzsche seems to have been that Schopenhauer was continually saying ' no.' He agreed to nothing, he had no reverence for anything. Plato and Kant were the only philosophers to whom he granted an honorable position, and he was particularly concerned with the abuse of Hegel. He said what he meant in an emphatic manner, and most of what he said was objectionable to the people who heard him. This was exactly the attitude which met with Nietzsche's approval. He had no sympathy for half-measures, nor for a man who could agree with his predecessors; and the highest tribute that he paid to Schopenhauer concerns this very independence.[1]

> *" Was er lehrte ist abgethan,*
> *Was er lebte, wird bleiben stahn :*
> *Seht ihn nur an !*
> *Niemandem war er unterthan ! "*

Sec. 2. Hegel and the Hegelians.

In 1886, when Nietzsche was preparing a complete edition of his published works, he condemned the Hegelian spirit in *Die Geburt der Tragödie.* That a disciple of Schopenhauer should also be a follower of Hegel, seems almost a contradiction in terms; and Nietzsche himself, during the period in question, would undoubtedly have found it so. He needed the clearer perspective afforded by distance in order to recognize the Hegelian element in his own work; and its very lack of definite outline is a tribute to the all-pervasive influence exercised by Hegel upon the philosophic thought of the nineteenth century. Even Nietzsche, an avowed member of a rival school, could not altogether escape it.

[1] VIII, p. 336.

The most striking instances of Hegelianism are confined to the notes published by Frau Förster-Nietzsche. Here one finds some discussion of the origin of the world, which is explained as the creation of the intellect.[1] At the beginning there was only eternal being, and this, by means of the idea, changed into becoming. Such speculation evidently had no place in *Die Geburt der Tragödie* nor in *Unzeitgemässe Betrachtungen;* and Nietzsche not only did not publish them, but did not even put them into systematic form. In the books just mentioned, the affirmation of the necessity of strife and opposition seems to be essentially Hegelian. In his later writings, too, the same theory, though in a less Hegelian form, is still present. The negative and contradictory element is given great importance. Nevertheless, emphasize Nietzsche's Hegelian affinities as one may, they were not of great moment in the formation of his own views.[2]

The case is somewhat different with the followers of Hegel, who turned their attention more entirely to concrete problems. In the field of religion, especially, the most radical of them are to be regarded as his predecessors. In spite of his impatience with Strauss, his own attitude toward religion and especially Christianity, would hardly have been what it was, had it not been for the writings of Strauss and Feuerbach. With the reduction of the essence of religion to morality, they helped to pave the way for Nietzsche's more extreme views. From them and from the French philosophers of the Illumination he gained much of his general attitude toward questions of this nature.

Sec. 3. The Materialistic and Neo-Kantian Movements.

The whole trend of philosophic thought during the second half of this century has been away from speculation, properly speaking, and in the direction of science. There has been a tendency to confine ultimate theories to those presuppositions necessary to science which, though abstract in themselves, yet never lose their connection with the concrete. The Materialists and

---

[1] IX, pp. 164–166.

[2] Riehl (p. 109) calls the scheme, *Herrenmoral, Sclavenmoral,* a bad Hegelian historical construction.

the Neo-Kantians share between them the honor, if it be one, of this revolt from metaphysical idealism ; and Nietzsche's thought, so far as this general position goes, was akin to both movements. In a sense, all individualism is a form of sensationalism, inasmuch as both limit a man to his own mental states, without any recourse to a world reason or substance for further explanation. There can be no universal knowledge, no universal standards, because the individual can never get beyond himself.   Of course it is possible to trace this position back to Protagoras, and several writers have pointed out the connection between Nietzsche and the Sophists ; but there is no need of going so far afield.   The philosophy of the last fifty years furnishes plenty of examples of this standpoint ; and with all due respect to Nietzsche's Grecian proclivities, he is much more likely to have been influenced by his contemporaries than by the ancients.

Another likeness between Nietzsche and the Neo-Kantians especially is his positivism.   Metaphysics is an error, once universally accepted, but now seen in its true light.   It has had its share in the formation of the human reason, and has played its part well, but the time of its usefulness is long gone by ; and, if it will not step aside of its own will, it must be pushed out of the way.   Nietzsche, to be sure, went a step further than most of the Neo-Kantians would have been willing to go.   He not only denied the possibility of a metaphysics, but he even hinted that the reason for man's necessary ignorance upon such topics lay less in the limitation of the human reason than in the absence of anything to be known.   Why lament the unknowableness of the *Ding-an-sich*, when there is no *Ding-an-sich* to know?   Metaphysics is false, but it is more aptly described as meaningless, because it deals with non-entities.

Perhaps the most exact parallel to be found for Nietzsche's work is that of Max Stirner (Kaspar Schmidt), who does not strictly belong to either of the schools in question.[1]   In his book,

---

[1] It has seemed unnecessary to discuss the question of the extent of Paul Rée's influence upon Nietzsche.   The importance of their intercourse has been variously estimated, but Nietzsche's note-books show that he already held the views common to both, before their publication by Rée.

Der Einzige und sein Eigenthum, published in 1845, Stirner glorifies the individual to the utmost extent. He questions truth,
denies the value of religion, custom, morality, everything made
near and dear by tradition, and almost out-Nietzsches Nietzsche,
although there is no evidence to show that Nietzsche was acquainted with his work. The resemblance between them has not
been unobserved; Robert Schellwien, in particular, has enlarged
upon it, perhaps overestimated it.[1] Upon close examination the
similarity is not so great as one might be led to think at first.
The standpoint of the two is fundamentally different. Stirner,
for instance, makes his vaunted egoism a synonym for self-indul-
gence of the most sensual sort. Religion, the state, all restraints
are to be discarded, not because they hinder the highest development of the individual, but because they make it harder for every
man to get whatever he happens to want. Sympathy and brotherly
love may be indulged, because they give their possessor pleasure.
There is no suggestion of an ideal, whether stern or beneficent.
Nietzsche's position is as far as possible from all this. As Professor Seth says, whatever may be thought of his ideals, he was
always in pursuit of an ideal of some kind.[2] The resemblance
between Nietzsche and Stirner is confined to the critical attitude
assumed by both toward the prevailing opinions and institutions.
They might have agreed as to what must be destroyed; but the
beginning of the work of construction would have put them at
sword's points in an instant.

Sec. 4. Literary Affinities.

Apart from Max Stirner, Nietzsche's predecessors and fellows
in individualistic egoism are to be found in the ranks of the *lit-
térateurs* rather than among philosophers. His maxim, "nothing
is true, everything is allowed," gives the keynote to his final
position, and this standpoint is not at all an uncommon one, but
is almost universal among the so-styled decadents. Poetry,
romance, and the drama are full of it. In England and America
the tone is not so prevalent, and when present is not pronounced,

---

[1] *Max Stirner und Friedrich Nietzsche. Erscheinungen des modernen Geistes
und des Wesen des Menschen.*

[2] *Blackwood's Magazine,* October, 1897, p. 483.

but on the continent its devotees are found almost everywhere. The French symbolists belong to their number; Baudelaire and Verlaine, Maeterlinck and Ibsen, singly or collectively, dominate them all.   Some of these men are mystics, it is true, and they differ greatly among themselves; but at bottom they are all of one faith, and Nietzsche belongs to the same brotherhood.   The loosening of the bonds of conventional morality, the deification of the individual, the assumption that no price is too great to pay for the development of an independent personality—this whole attitude Nietzsche shares with many others.   It was not peculiar to him, although he gave it its philosophic form.   There is not the slightest reason for supposing that Nietzsche was greatly influenced by the writers in question, or even that he was acquainted with the work of most of them; but the whole trend of thought was in the air, and the very fact that he was prone to think for himself made it attractive to him.   He could not get away from the time in which he lived; no amount of independence will enable a man to do that.   In the eighteenth century, Nietzsche would have been a materialist, and perhaps have disputed the laurels of La Mettrie and Holbach.   In this age, the lines followed by the literary movements were more attractive to him than those of philosophy proper, and his own philosophy might have been adopted by the whole literary school.

One of the most striking resemblances between Nietzsche on the one side and these poets and dramatists on the other, is difficult to describe, because it is so evasive in character.   That the general atmosphere of all their work is alike, is easy to feel, but it is almost impossible to formulate in words any specific basis for the feeling.   The men all breathed the same intellectual air, they were all more or less *fin de siècle*, they were all considered reprobates by the people whom Nietzsche called "the good and just," and perhaps some of them deserved to be; but they were artists every one, and to the ideals they set up we owe *Also sprach Zarathustra.*   Other philosophers have written books worthy to be called literature from the stylistic standpoint, but no one else in this century has written philosophy that is at the same time poetry.

Sec. 5. The Significance of Nietzsche's Philosophy.

In many subjects doubtless Nietzsche's most ardent admirers would hardly claim for him any great originality. In the fields of art, music, and literature—he left much scattered criticism, but he raised no new questions, and proposed no original answers to those already current. In æsthetics, his theory of the origin of Greek tragedy and of the two artistic forces was certainly new ; but it was of so arbitrary a character that its novelty remained one of the strongest points in its favor. In fact, the claim that Nietzsche has added something of permanent value to the history of thought must rest entirely upon his ethics ; and since practically all his original work upon this subject is comprised within the third period, his earlier writings need not be considered here. The metaphysical basis for the ethics is not of much importance. Nietzsche's emphasis upon the will is always from the standpoint of ethics, not of metaphysics. It is the will as manifested in the actual life of humanity ; and though its sphere is extended until it becomes an explanatory principle for the universe, one always feels that Nietzsche was less in earnest, as soon as he left the field of human activity. He never took the trouble to complete his more ultimate theories ; and since he warmly denied having any, he was doubtless right in neglecting them, whenever he could.

The ethics built upon this foundation is both critical and constructive. The former portion is generally regarded as unproven, but fortunately the constructive part of the theory, which is concerned mainly with the moral ideal, is independent of the criticism. Here, if one ignores the Over-man, which has no vital relation to the end as exemplified in conduct, a striking difference of method is observable between Nietzsche's treatment of the latter subject and that of most other ethical writers. For while such writers accept the moral phenomena as something given, and base their doctrines of the *summum bonum* upon the distinctions between good and bad actually made by mankind, Nietzsche proposes not only to explain morality but to construct it. He denies entirely the validity of universal consent, the consciousness of the race, or whatever else may be called in to vouch for the existence of the

phenomena to be explained, and maintains that the accepted views are false.   Instead of seeking to show that his moral end, the will for power, is really present in all moral action, he seems rather to set up his end and then make an arbitrary code of morals to agree with it.   Of course no one accepts the whole mass of moral judgments, but necessarily chooses certain distinctions and discards others as temporary or ill-founded, and it might be urged that Nietzsche did no more than this.   Still, when reference is made neither to experience nor to the testimony of consciousness, some argument in addition to assertion seems to be needed, and it must be admitted that Nietzsche afforded no confirmation of his theory.   He took it for granted that the man of insight would agree with him, and he was not much concerned with the rest of the human race.

One of the most striking characteristics of the type of conduct thus arbitrarily set up is its extreme individualism.   There is not the slightest suggestion of a social ideal.   The individual is all in all and is never to be subordinated to the whole.   In Nietzsche's ethics there are no difficult questions to be decided regarding the conflict between the good of the individual and that of society, because the latter is held to be deserving of no consideration.   The end in general is the production and development of mighty individuals; the end for every strong man is his own development, his own supremacy without regard to others.   The weak can hardly be said to have an end.   Unless a man has fighting blood, and insight enough to give his instincts full play, he is nothing but material upon which the strong may exercise their power.   Only the best of the race are worthy of the new morality; it is an ideal for the few, never to become common, never to be degraded by acceptance on the part of the herd.   Not only is the individual the judge of good and evil, but he is also the ethical end.   He is himself the justification of the universe, and his power may and should extend as far as he can make it.   The more power he has, the greater the number of weaker men he can bring under his subjection, the higher is the type of morality to which he has attained.

Whether such a theory is felt to be adequate or not, it must

be admitted that Nietzsche has avoided one pitfall that lies in
wait for the unwary advocate of individualism. He never for-
gets that he is concerned with a man among men, and not with
the inhabitant of a desert island. He does not deny that mankind is naturally social and sympathetic, that to share the pleasure
and pain of another is a part of human character, that the desire to relieve the suffering and promote the happiness of others
is often present and is responsible for its share of activity. He
admits the existence of all the sympathetic and social feelings,
but bids the great man restrain them, if he can, destroy them utterly, for they are unworthy of him. They will drag him down
to the level of the masses. If he is pitiful, he will be also weak,
and for the weak there is no help nor hope. The great individual is possible only while he remains unyielding.

It is evident that living examples of Nietzsche's ethical ideal
were more often to be found in the past than they are at present ;
and his demand that we go back to the simpler emotions and instincts of an earlier and more primitive age has gained him the
epithet of the modern Rousseau. Nevertheless, although there is
a certain likeness between the two men, the differences are greater
than the resemblances. They both protested against the prevailing intellectual and moral tendencies of their times. They both
pointed out the evil effects of civilization, and were at one in
preaching a return to nature. Moreover, they both put their
trust in feeling rather than in intellect, and looked upon reason
as an unsafe guide. The great difference between them lies in
the object that animated their protests against their surroundings.
Rousseau dreamed of a gentle savage, ruled by sympathy and
' innocent self-love,' open to all the promptings of a natural religion, the representative of a kinder, more humane type than the
product of civilization. Nietzsche's savage would have scorned
so weak a creature, and have trodden him under foot at the first
opportunity. Rousseau longed for the very qualities that Nietzsche most despised. Their protests were directed against totally
different tendencies ; and when one remembers how far apart
their standpoints are, even the actual resemblances seem super-
ficial.

It is a long way from the return to nature to the struggle for life and the survival of the fittest, but Nietzsche has been compared to Darwin almost as often as to Rousseau. His philosophy has been called ' Darwinism gone mad ' ; and even if this phrase expresses more than the truth, it cannot be denied that evolutionary elements are present. In any former century, Nietzsche's theories could hardly have taken exactly the same form ; the same value could hardly have been given to the struggle of the individual. Nietzsche's view of the matter was entirely from the ethical standpoint, however, and the struggle was not for preservation or reproduction, but for power. It was a transference to the sphere of human action of the unceasing warfare of the organic world with which Darwin had made men familiar. Apart from this, the system is not really evolutionary in its tendencies. There is no thought of development, of the selection and preservation of favorable characteristics. The struggle is often not so well adapted to preserve life as a quieter and more slavish mode of existence would be. The general warfare is not viewed as a scientific fact, but as an ethical end to be attained. It is not everywhere present, but it ought to be.

In fact, just as Nietzsche's system is not naturalism, so it is not Darwinism ; the one name that can be given to it without qualification is egoism. Here again, however, it must be clearly distinguished from egoism in the most commonly accepted sense of the term. As has already been said, there is no denial of the existence of altruistic instincts but instead a refusal to justify them. Their existence is admitted and deplored. It is true that Nietzsche attempts to show that many so-called altruistic acts are at basis due to selfish motives, but he does not place them all in this category. Sympathy, unselfishness, sacrifice, all exist—they are only too common. But until a man has conquered them, he has no share in the higher morality. Nietzsche treats the egoistic impulses ethically, not psychologically. Instead of showing that they govern all action, he transforms them into an ideal.

Yet egoistic as his end of conduct is, it is strongly antihedonistic. The instincts, even the most sensuous, are to have full play, the earth is not to be despised, there is to be no self-repression ; but the end of the indulgence is strength, not pleasure, and the common characteristic of all enjoyment lies in its expression of free activity. Nietzsche's higher man does not restrain his appetites, because such subjection to legal or moral law would be unworthy of him, fit only for a slave. A lord may do as he likes, but his one all-ruling desire is for power ; enjoyment is a purely secondary consideration. Hedonistic elements are present, as they must be, at least implicitly, in every treatment of the ethical end, but the system cannot be called a form of hedonism. The other elements are of too great importance.

From one point of view, indeed, one might question whether Nietzsche's ethics could be called entirely egoistic. So long as the end as embodied in conduct is considered, there seems no doubt that the system is egoism pure and simple ; but a disturbing element enters with the Over-man. The end of the higher man's life is something still higher than himself, a mystical being, whose production demands and justifies the greatest sacrifices. One should will to die that the Over-man may live. Yet the way to do this is not by destroying the egoistic part of one's nature. Sympathy with others, old and dear beliefs, cherished aims and ambitions that are found to be false when judged by the new standard, these are what must die. At all costs the egoist must become more egoistic still, if he would help to bring about the Over-man. He must sacrifice himself, but only that side of his nature that finds expression in self-sacrifice. Moreover, whatever the Over-man may be, he is certainly an egoist *par excellence*. To die for the Over-man is to die for the sake of an egoistic ideal.

When all is said then, what is the significance of Nietzsche's account of morality ? If one omits all the critical and extraneous additions, perhaps will for power, which is self-assertion, expresses the essence of the doctrine. The value of such a theory, however, has been variously estimated. Its weakest point is its arbitrariness. To a certain extent an attempt is made to justify it by showing that the current morality is essentially degenerate, that it is at once the result and the cause of weakness ; but the proofs for the proposed substitute are inadequate, and the final appeal is always to the delicate discrimination of the aristocrat. A morality that is to apply only to a favored few of the race might seem at first to require less justification than a more universal system, but in reality it requires more; for it must justify the acceptance of such an arbitrary division, and this Nietzsche never pretended to do. The validity of a class-morality was one of his assumptions. Without regard to the nature of the ideal setup, which attracts some people and antagonizes others, and which like all ideals can neither be proven nor disproven, Nietzsche's ethics is narrow, and therefore inadequate, arbitrary, and therefore unconvincing.

Yet, on the other hand, there is much to be said in its favor. In the first place, it supplies a distinct want in the mental atmosphere of the time. In an age whose watchword in politics is democracy, and in ethics self-sacrifice, it is well to be reminded that aristocracy and self-assertion are not synonymous with evil. Even an ideal democracy would hardly be an unmixed blessing, while its actual form leaves still more to be desired. Self-sacrifice, if consistently adhered to, results in a personality that ought to be sacrificed, and the sooner the better. If life is to be maintained at all, there must be some self-assertion; and much more is necessary, if the life is to be worthy of maintenance. Humility and abnegation have had more than their due share of glory. In putting aside the old warlike ideals, and in finding others more generous and more humane, there has been a tendency, perhaps, to confuse values, and to forget that the virtues of the soldier were incomplete, but not therefore vices. It is still worth while to hear the claims of courage advocated by a man who believes what he says. A utilitarian civilization needs to be reminded that lack of strength in the individual is not to be compensated by any amount of general comfort, that a vigorous personality is more to be desired than self-effacement, and that pain is not so bad as the want of power to endure it. That Nietzsche's own ideal was narrow and one-sided is undoubtedly true; but this is not surprising when one remembers that the view he opposes is also only part of the complete truth. Neither self-sacrifice nor self-assertion, regarded in isolation, furnish a sufficient content for the moral ideal. But self-assertion, in a certain sense, is an element of it, and it is Nietzsche's merit to have given this principle emphatic expression.

Such a supplementing of current views, however valuable it may be, does not constitute Nietzsche's main contribution to philosophic thought. To the writer's mind, this is to be found in the special form of his egoism. The main difference between his system and those of other ethical writers lies in the new valuation which he gives to the egoistic instincts, in the fact that he regards them not merely as psychological present, but as expressing the ethical end of life. In this new point of view lies his importance for ethics, and here the claim for his originality has the best basis. Of course, there have been suggestions of such views before, especially in Max Stirner; but nowhere else has the theory found philosophic expression. Narrow, arbitrary, incomplete as Nietzsche's system is, it presents a new form of egoism, which is perfectly distinct from that of its predecessors.

BIBLIOGRAPHY.

1. NIETZSCHE'S WORKS.

The standard edition of Nietzsche's works is that published by C. G. Naumann at Leipsic in 1895 and the following years. This consists of two parts : the first, comprising eight volumes, contains the books already published by Nietzsche, as well as two or three that he left ready for the press. The second part consists of four volumes, made up, for the most part, of selections from his note books. The following table of first editions refers only to the first division :

Vol. I. 1. *Die Geburt der Tragödie*[1] was first published in 1872, and is made up of two lectures, *Das Griechische Musikdrama* and *Sokrates und die Tragödie*, both delivered at Bâle in the winter of 1870. The second of the two was privately printed for circulation among friends.

   2. *Unzeitgemässe Betrachtungen.*[2]

    (*a*) *David Strauss, der Bekenner und der Schriftsteller.* First edition in 1873

    (*b*) *Vom Nutzen und Nachtheil der Historie für das Leben.* 1874.

    (*c*) *Schopenhauer als Erzieher.* 1874.

    (*d*) *Richard Wagner in Bayreuth.* 1876.

Vols. II and III *Menschliches allzu Menschliches. Ein Buch für Freie Geister.* The first volume[3] was published under the present title in 1878, after the first title chosen for it, *Die Pflugschar*, had been discarded. Of the second volume,[4] the *Erste Abtheilung* appeared in 1879, with the title, *Menschliches allzu Menschliches, Ein Buch für Freie Geister. Anhang : Vermischte Meinungen und Sprüche.* The *Zweite Abtheilung* appeared in 1880, as *Der Wanderer und sein Schatten.* In 1886 the two parts were united to form the second volume of *Menschliches allzu Menschliches.*

Vol. IV. *Morgenröte.*[5] 1881. It was written under the title of *Die Pflugschar*, but not so printed.

----

[1] *Werke*, Vol. I, *Nachbericht*, p. ii.
[2] *Ibid.*, pp. viii–xiii.
[3] *Ibid.*, Vol. II, *Nachbericht*, pp. i and ii.
[4] *Ibid.*, Vol. III, *Nachbericht*, pp. i and ii.
[5] *Werke*, Vol. IV, *Nachbericht*, p. 1.

Vol. V. *Die fröhliche Wissenschaft.*[1] 1882. The first edition contained the *Vorspiel, Scherz, List, und Rache,* and four books. In 1887, the *Vorrede,* the Fifth Book, and the *Lieder des Prinzen Vogelfrei,* were added.

Vol. VI. *Also sprach Zarathustra.*[2] *Ein Buch für Alle und Keinen.* The first part was published in April, 1883, the second in September, 1883, the third in April, 1884, each under the present title of the whole. The fourth was privately printed for circulation among friends in 1885, and first given to the public in March, 1892. The first edition containing all four parts was published in July, 1892.

Vol. VII. 1. *Jenseits von Gut und Böse.*[3] 1886.

2. *Zur Geneologie der Moral.*[4] 1887.

Vol. VIII. 1. *Der Fall Wagner*[5] 1888.

2. *Götzendämmerung,*[6] published in 1889, after Nietzsche's illness. The first title chosen for it was *Müssiggang eines Psychologen.*

3. *Nietsche contra Wagner.*[7] This was printed in 1889, but on account of Nietzsche's illness was not given to the public. It is composed of selections from his earlier works, often abbreviated, with here and there additions and changes.

4. *Der Antichrist,*[8] not before published. It was to form the first book of Nietzsche's chief work, the plan for which was as follows :

Der Wille zur Macht. Versuch einer Umwerthung aller Werthe.

Der Antichrist. Versuch einer Kritik des Christenthums. (Erstes Buch.)

Der freie Geist. Kritik der Philosophie als einer nihilistichen Bewegung. (Zweites Buch.)

Der Immoralist. Kritik der verhängnissvollsten Art von Unwissenheit, der Moral. (Drittes Buch.)

Dionysus, Philosophie der ewigen Wiederkunft. (Viertes Buch.)

5. *Gedichte,*[9] like 3 and 4, not before published.

---

[1] *Ibid.,* Vol. V, *Nachbericht,* pp. i and ii.

[2] *Ibid.,* Vol. VI, *Nachbericht,* p. iii.

[3] *Ibid.,* Vol. VII, *Nachbericht,* p. i.

[4] *Ibid.,* p. ii.

[5] *Ibid.,* Vol. VIII, *Nachbericht,* p. i.

[6] *Ibid.,* pp. i and ii.

[7] *Ibid.,* p. ii.

[8] *Ibid.,* p. iii.

[9] *Ibid.,* p. iv.

2. COMMENTARIES.

Achelis, Th. *Friedrich Nietzsche*, Hamburg, 1895.

Adler, Georg. *Friedrich Nietzsche, der Social-Philosoph der Aristokratie, Nord und Sud*, vol. 56, March, 1891, pp. 224–240.

Andreas-Salome, Lou. *Friedrich Nietzsche in seinen Werken*, Vienna, 1894.

Antrim, Ernest and Dr. Heinrich Goebel. *Friedrich Nietzsche's Uebermensch, The Monist*, July, 1899, pp. 563–571.

Bakewell, Chas. M. *The Teachings of Friedrich Nietzsche, The International Journal of Ethics*, IX, 4, April, 1899, pp. 314–331.

√ **Bellaique, Camille.** *Un Problème Musical. Le Cas Wagner, Revue des deux Mondes*, March 1, 1892, pp. 221–227.

Bernhard, Johannes. *Friedrich Nietzsche Apostata*, Lübeck, 1898.

Brandes, Georg. *Menschen und Werke*, Frankfurt, 1895; essay entitled *Friedrich Nietzsche*, pp. 137–224.

Essays. Moderne Bahnbrecher, Leipsic, 1897; essays entitled *Friedrich Nietzsche*, pp. 97–157. (With the exception of verbal changes, possibly due to the translator, this essay is the same as that in *Menschen und Werke*, save that it omits some letters found there.)

Aristokratischer Radicalismus. Eine Abhandlung über Friedrich Nietzsche, Deutsche Rundschau, April, 1890, vol. 63, pp. 52–89 (the same essay as that given above).

Carus, Dr. Paul. *Immorality as Philosophical Principle. A Study of the Philosophy of Friedrich Nietzsche, The Monist*, July, 1899, pp. 572–616.

Cron, Bernhard (Peter Gast). Prefaces to the second edition of *Unzeitgemässe Betrachtungen* and *Also sprach Zarathustra*, Leipsic, 1893.

Duboc, Julius. *Anti-Nietztche*, Dresden, 1897.

Eisner, Kurt. *Psychopathia spiritualis. Friedrich Nietzsche und die Apostel der Zukunft*, Leipsic, 1892.

Everett, C. C. '*Beyond Good and Evil,*' *A Study of the Philosophy of Friedrich Nietzsche, The New World*, December, 1898, pp. 684–703.

Falkenfeld, Max. *Marx und Nietzsche*, Leipsic, 1899.

Förster-Nietzsche, Elisabeth. *Das Leben Friedrich Nietzsche's,*

Vol. I, Leipsic, 1895; Vol. II, Leipsic, 1897. (Another volume is to be added.)

Preface to the German translation of *La Philosophie de Nietzsche,* by **Henri Lichtenberger,** Dresden, 1899.

Fuchs, George Friedrich. *Friedrich Nietzsche. Sein Leben und seine Lehre mit besonderer Berücksichtigung seiner Stellung zum Christentum,* Stuttgart, 1897.

Gallwitz, Hans. *Friedrich Nietzsche. Ein Lebensbild,* Dresden and Leipsic, 1898.

Gast, Peter (pseudonym of Bernhard Cron). Prefaces to the second edition of *Unzeitgemässe Betrachtungen* and *Also sprach Zarathustra,* Leipsic, 1893.

Goebel, Dr. Heinrich, and **Ernest Antrim.** *Friedrich Nietsche's Uebermensch, The Monist,* July, 1899, pp. 563–571.

Grimm, Ed. *Das Problem Friedrich Nietzsche's,* Berlin, 1899.

Grot, Nikolaus. *Nietzsche und Tolstoi,* Berlin, 1898.

Grote. *Moral Systems of Tolstoi and Nietzsche, Public Opinion,* 14: 621, April 1, 1893.

Hannson, Ola. *Friedrich Nietzsche. Seine Persönlichkeit und sein System,* Leipsic.

v. Hartmann, Eduard. *Ethische Studien,* essay entitled *Nietzsche's neue Moral,* pp. 34–69.

Henne am Rhyn, Dr. Otto. *Anti-Zarathustra. Gedanken über Friedrich Nietzsche's Hauptwerke,* Altenburg, 1899.

Hillebrand. *Zeiten, Völker, und Menschen,* Vol. II, three essays: *Einiges über den Verfall der deutschen Sprache und der deutschen Gesinnung. (Bei Gelegenheit einer Schrift von Dr. Fried. Nietzsche gegen David Strauss),* pp. 291–310; *Ueber historisches Wissen und historischen Sinn,* pp. 314–338, and *Schopenhauer und das deutsche Publikum,* pp. 353–366, Berlin, 1895.

Horneffer, Dr. Ernst. *Nietzsche's Lehre von der ewigen Wiederkunft und deren bisherigen Veröffentlichung,* Leipsic, 1900.

Vorträge über Nietzsche. Versuch einer Wiedergabe seiner Gedanken, Göttingen, 1900.

Huneker, James. *Mezzotints in Modern Music,* New York, 1899; essay entitled *Richard Strauss and Nietzsche,* pp. 141–159.

Kaatz, Hugo. *Die Weltanschauung Friedrich Nietzsche's,* Dresden and Leipsic, 1899.

Kaftan, Julius. *Das Christenthum und Nietzsche's Herrenmoral,* Berlin, 1897.

Kalina, Paul E. *Fundament und Einheit in Friedrich Nietzsche's Philosophie,* Leipsic.

Krausz, Károly. *Nietzsche und seine Weltanschauung.*

Kreibig, Josef C. (Dr. Laurentius). *Krapotkins Morallehre und deren Beziehungen zu Nietzsche,* Dresden and Leipsic, 1896.

Kretzer, Eugen. *Friedrich Nietzsche. Nach persönlichen Erinnerungen und aus seinen Schriften,* Leipsic and Frankfurt, 1895.

Laurentius, Dr. (pseudonym of Josef C. Kreibig). *Krapotkins Morallehre und deren Beziehungen zu Nietzsche,* Dresden and Leipsic, 1896.

Lichtenberger, Henri. *La Philosophie de Nietzsche,* Paris, 1899. *Friedrich Nietzsche. Aphorismes et Fragments Choisis,* Paris, 1899. *Quelques Lettres Inédites, avec Introduction, Cosmopolis,* May, 1897, Vol. 6, pp. 460–474.

Maxi (pseudonym of Maximilian Stein). *Nietzsche-Kritik,* Zürich, 1895.

v. Meysenbug, Malwida. *Der Lebensabend einer Idealistin.*

Moeller-Bruck, Arth. *Die moderne Literatur in Gruppen und Einzeldarstellungen.* Vol. I, *Tschandala Nietzsche,* Berlin, 1899.

Naumann, Gust. *Zarathustra-Commentar,* Leipsic, 1. Thl. 1899, 2. Thl. 1900.

Nicoladoni, Dr. Alex. *Jenseits von Gut und Böse! Vortrag geh. in der Gesellschaft der Namenlosen in Linz. im März. 1898;* Linz, 1899.

Nordau, Max. *Degeneration,* translation of the 2d German edition, New York, 1895; essay entitled *Friedrich Nietzsche,* pp. 415–472.

Przybyszewski, Stanilaus. *Zur Psychologie des Individuums. I Chopin und Nietzsche,* Berlin, 1892.

Riehl, Alois. *Friedrich Nietzsche. Der Künstler und der Denker,* Stuttgart, 1898.

Ritschl, Otto. *Nietzsche's Welt- und Lebensanschauung in ihrer Entstehung und Entwicklung,* Freiburg and Leipsic, 1897.

Rode, Albert. *Hauptmann und Nietzsche,* Hamburg, 1897.

Rohde, Erwin. *Afterphilologie. Sendschreiben eines Philologen an Richard Wagner,* Leipsic, 1872 (reply to v. Wilamowitz-Möllendorf's *Zukunftsphilologie*).

Runze, Geo. *Friedrich Nietzsche als Theologe und als Antichrist,* Berlin, 1896.

Rzewuski, Stanilaus. *La Philosophie de Nietzsche, Cosmopolis,* Oct., 1898, pp. 134–145.

v. Salis-Marschlins, Meta. *Philosoph und Edelmensch, Ein Betrag zur Charakteristik Friedrich Nietzsche's,* Leipsic, 1897.

Schellwien, Robert. *Max Stirner und Friedrich Nietzsche, Erscheinungen des modernen Geistes und des Wesen des Menschen,* Leipsic, 1892.
Nietzsche und seine Weltanschauung. Eine kritische Studie, Leipsic, 1897.

Schiller, F. C. S. *A philosophic Mr. Hyde, The Nation,* Vol. 62, p. 459.

Sehuster, L. *Nietzsche's Moral Philosophie,* Göttingen, 1897.

Seth Pringle, Pattison, A. *Friedrich Nietzsche : His Life and Works, Blackwood's Magazine,* Oct., 1897, pp. 476–493.
The Opinions of Friedrich Nietzsche, The Critical Review, May, 1898, pp. 727–750.

Schuré, Edouard. *L'Individualisme et l'Anarchie en Littérature. Frédéric Nietzsche et sa philosophie, Revue des deux Mondes,* Aug. 15, 1895, pp. 775–805.

Stein, Ludwig. *Friedrich Nietzsche's Weltanschauung und ihre Gefahren,* Berlin, 1893.

Stein, Maximilian (Maxi). *Nietzsche-Kritik,* Zürich, 1895.

Steiner, Rudolf. *Friedrich Nietzsche. Ein Kämpfer gegen seine Zeit,* Weimar, 1895.

Tienes, Georg A. *Nietzsche's Stellung zu den Grundfragen der Ethik genetisch dargestellt,* Bern, 1899.

Tille, Alexander. *Von Darwin bis Nietzsche,* Leipsic, 1895.

Tönnies, Ferdinand. *Der Nietzsche-Kultus,* Leipsic, 1897.

Türck, Hermann. *Friedrich Nietzsche und seine philosophische Irrwege,* Jena and Leipsic, 1891.

Unger, Fritz. *Friedrich Nietzsche's Träumen und Sterben*, Munich, 1900.

Valbert, G. *Le Docteur Friedrich Nietzsche et ses Griefs contre la société moderne, Revue des deux Mondes*, October, 1892, pp. 677–689.

Wagner, Richard. *Gesammte Schriften*, Vol. IX, p. 350.

Waldmann, Wilhelm. *Friedrich Nietzsche. Ein Blick in seine Werke vom Standpunkte eines Laien*, Leipsic, 1898.

Wallace, W. *Lectures and Essays on Natural Theology*, Oxford, 1898 ; essays entitled *Nietzsche's Criticism of Mortality,''* pp. 511–529, and *Nietzsche's "Thus Spake Zarathustra,''* pp. 530–541.

Weigand, Wilhelm. *Friedrich Nietzsche. Ein psychologischer Versuch*, Munich, 1893.

v. Wilamowitz-Möllendorf, Ulrich. *Zukunftsphilologie / eine Erwidrung auf Friedrich Nietzsche's "Geburt der Tragödie,''* Berlin, 1872.

Zukunftsphilologie. Zweites Stück, eine Erwidrung auf die Rettungsversuchung für Friedrich Nietzsche's "Geburt der Tragödie,'' Berlin, 1893.

Wilhelmi, T. H. *Thomas Carlyle und Friedrich Nietzsche. Wie sie Gott suchten und was für einen Gott sie fanden*, Göttingen, 1897.

de Wyzewa, T. *La Jeunesse de Frédéric Nietzsche, Revue des deux Mondes*, February 1, 1896, pp. 688–699.

L'Amitié de Frédéric Nietzsche et Richard Wagner, Ibid., May 15, 1897, pp. 457–468.

Zerbst, Max. *Nein und Ja* (an answer to Türck's *Friedrich Nietzsche und seine philosophische Irrwege*), Leipsic, 1892.

Ziegler, Prof. Dr. Theobald. *Vorkämpfer des Jahrhunderts : Eine Sammlung von Biographien*, Vol. I, Berlin.

Zoccoli, E. G. *Friedrich Nietzsche*, Modena, 1898.

Printed in the United States
130691LV00015B/349/A

9 781430 496755